NATIONAL ACADEMIES

Sciences
Engineering
Medicine

MW01074766

Toward a 21st Century National Data Infrastructure: Mobilizing Information for the Common Good

Robert M. Groves, Thomas Mesenbourg,
and Michael Siri, *Editors*

Panel on the Scope, Components, and
Key Characteristics of a 21st Century
Data Infrastructure

Committee on National Statistics

Division of Behavioral and Social
Sciences and Education

Consensus Study Report

NATIONAL ACADEMIES PRESS 500 Fifth Street, NW Washington, DC 20001

This activity was supported by award number SES-2114583 between the National Academy of Sciences and the National Science Foundation. Support for the work of the Committee on National Statistics is provided by a consortium of federal agencies through a grant from the National Science Foundation, a National Agricultural Statistics Service cooperative agreement, and several individual contracts. Any opinions, findings, conclusions, or recommendations expressed in this publication do not necessarily reflect the views of any organization or agency that provided support for the project.

International Standard Book Number-13: 978-0-309-69274-8
International Standard Book Number-10: 0-309-69274-1
Digital Object Identifier: https://doi.org/10.17226/26688
Library of Congress Control Number: 2022950596

This publication is available from the National Academies Press, 500 Fifth Street, NW, Keck 360, Washington, DC 20001; (800) 624-6242 or (202) 334-3313; http://www.nap.edu.

Suggested citation: National Academies of Sciences, Engineering, and Medicine. 2023. *Toward a 21st Century National Data Infrastructure: Mobilizing Information for the Common Good.* Washington, DC: The National Academies Press. https://doi.org/10.17226/26688.

The **National Academy of Sciences** was established in 1863 by an Act of Congress, signed by President Lincoln, as a private, nongovernmental institution to advise the nation on issues related to science and technology. Members are elected by their peers for outstanding contributions to research. Dr. Marcia McNutt is president.

The **National Academy of Engineering** was established in 1964 under the charter of the National Academy of Sciences to bring the practices of engineering to advising the nation. Members are elected by their peers for extraordinary contributions to engineering. Dr. John L. Anderson is president.

The **National Academy of Medicine** (formerly the Institute of Medicine) was established in 1970 under the charter of the National Academy of Sciences to advise the nation on medical and health issues. Members are elected by their peers for distinguished contributions to medicine and health. Dr. Victor J. Dzau is president.

The three Academies work together as the **National Academies of Sciences, Engineering, and Medicine** to provide independent, objective analysis and advice to the nation and conduct other activities to solve complex problems and inform public policy decisions. The National Academies also encourage education and research, recognize outstanding contributions to knowledge, and increase public understanding in matters of science, engineering, and medicine.

Learn more about the National Academies of Sciences, Engineering, and Medicine at **www.nationalacademies.org**.

PANEL ON THE SCOPE, COMPONENTS, AND KEY CHARACTERISTICS OF A 21ST CENTURY DATA INFRASTRUCTURE

ROBERT M. GROVES (*Chair*), Office of the Provost, Georgetown University
DANAH BOYD, Microsoft Research and Data & Society
ANNE C. CASE, School of Public and International Affairs, Princeton University, *Emeritus*
JANET M. CURRIE, School of Public and International Affairs; Co-Director, Center for Health and Wellbeing, Princeton University
ERICA L. GROSHEN, Cornell University School of Industrial and Labor Relations; Upjohn Institute for Employment Research
MARGARET C. LEVENSTEIN, Inter-university Consortium for Political and Social Research, University of Michigan
TED McCANN, American Idea Foundation
HELEN NISSENBAUM,[1] Cornell Tech, Cornell University
C. MATTHEW SNIPP, Department of Sociology, Stanford University
PATRICIA SOLÍS, School of Geographical Sciences and Urban Planning, Arizona State University

Staff

THOMAS MESENBOURG, *Study Director*
MICHAEL SIRI, *Associate Program Officer*
KATELYN STENGER, *Associate Program Officer*
JOSHUA LANG, *Senior Program Assistant*

---

[1]Resigned from panel on January 15, 2022.

Acknowledgments

This report is the product of contributions from many colleagues whom we thank for their time and expert guidance. The National Science Foundation (NSF) funded the project, and we are indebted to Daniel Goroff, Alan Tompkins, and Cheryl Eavey at NSF for valuable discussions and their support of the study.

To address gaps in the literature and to provide a forum for public comment, the panel convened two public workshop sessions in December 2021. Employees from statistical agencies in the United States and Europe, researchers, and private sector representatives described the impediments they confronted while attempting to blend nontraditional (usually private sector) data sources to improve national statistics.

The panel thanks the following individuals for presenting at these sessions: Cheryl Eavey (NSF) provided an overview of the project, highlighting areas where the panel's contributions could be especially impactful. Emilda Rivers (National Center for Science and Engineering Statistics) and Andrew Reamer (George Washington University) described federal statistical system initiatives that are examining issues similar to those that the panel studied. Ivan Deloach (Federal Geographic Data Committee), Mathew Shapiro (University of Michigan), and John Stevens (Federal Reserve Board of Governors) all offered valuable comments on these initiatives.

Antonio Chessa (Statistics Netherlands), Sarah Henry (U.K. Office of National Statistics), and Geoff Bowlby (Statistics Canada) offered their experiences in gathering and using private sector data in the production of national statistics, notably, describing the challenges they faced and overcame. Stephanie Studds (Census Bureau), Matt Gee (Brighthive), John

Haltiwanger (University of Maryland), and John Stevens (Federal Reserve Board of Governors) informed the panel on the use of private sector transaction data at U.S. statistical agencies. In a session on federal statistical agencies and nonprofits' use of private sector health data, Mary Bohman (Bureau of Economic Analysis), Brian Moyer (National Center for Health Statistics), and Niall Brennan (The Health Care Cost Institute) pointed out unique issues in obtaining and working with these data.

The workshop sessions concluded with a discussion of issues that arise when using private sector data for official statistics and research, especially the relationship between the data subject and data holder, as well as the changing legal, regulatory, and privacy landscape regarding private sector data. Nathan Persily (Stanford Law School) described his experiences with Social Science One and drafted legislation that could facilitate learning more about the benefits and limitations of private sector data. Salome Viljoen (Columbia Law School) provided the panel with an overview of the philosophical and legal underpinnings regarding notions of privacy. Panel member danah boyd offered her thoughts on the concept of "data as a gift" and how this theory informs data exchange agreements. Kadija Ferryman (Johns Hopkins Public Health), Frank Nothaft (CoreLogic), DJ Patil (Harvard University), Katherine Wallman (U.S. Office of Management and Budget [retired]), and Maurine Haver (Haver Analytics) provided excellent commentary on the issues set forth by Persily, Viljoen, and boyd.

The panel could not have conducted its work efficiently without the capable staff of the National Academies of Sciences, Engineering, and Medicine: Brian Harris-Kojetin, director of the Committee on National Statistics, provided institutional leadership and substantive contributions during meetings. Kirsten Sampson-Snyder, Division of Behavioral and Social Sciences and Education, expertly coordinated the review process, and Susan Debad and Bea Porter provided thorough final editing that improved the readability of the report for a wide audience. We also thank Rebecca Krone and Joshua Lang for well-organized and efficient logistical support of the panel's meetings, and Katelyn Stenger, who provided valuable research support throughout the project. On behalf of the panel, I thank the study directors, Thomas Mesenbourg and Michael Siri, for their excellent management of the panel's work. The quality and timeliness of this report would not have been possible without their contributions.

Finally, and most importantly, a note of appreciation is in order for my fellow panel members. This report reflects their collective expertise and commitment.

This Consensus Study Report was reviewed in draft form by individuals chosen for their diverse perspectives and technical expertise. The purpose of this independent review is to provide candid and critical comments that will assist the National Academies of Sciences, Engineering, and Medicine in making each published report as sound as possible and to ensure that it meets the institutional standards for quality, objectivity, evidence, and responsiveness to the study charge. The review comments and draft manuscript remain confidential to protect the integrity of the deliberative process.

The panel thanks the following individuals for their review of this report: Richard D. Alba (Department of Sociology, The Graduate Center, City University, New York), Claire McKay Bowen (Statistical Methods Group, Center on Labor, Human Services, and Population, Technology and Data Science, Urban Institute), Alan Butler (Office of President, Electronic Privacy Information Center, Washington, D.C.), Kathleen Cagney (Institute for Social Research and Department of Sociology, University of Michigan), Laura DeNardis (School of Communication, American University), Kenneth E. Poole (Office of the President, Center for Regional Economic Competitiveness, Arlington, VA), Kosali Simon (O'Neill School of Public and Environmental Affairs, Indiana University, Bloomington), and Timothy D. Wilson (Department of Psychology, University of Virginia).

Although the reviewers listed above provided many constructive comments and suggestions, they were not asked to endorse the conclusions, nor did they see the final draft of the report before its release. The review of the report was overseen by Cynthia Clark, independent consultant, Mclean, VA, and Kathleen Mullan Harris, Department of Sociology, University of North Carolina. Appointed by the National Research Council's Report Review Committee, they were responsible for making certain that the independent examination of this report was carried out per institutional procedures and that all review comments were carefully considered. Responsibility for the final content of the report rests entirely with the authoring panel and the National Academies of Sciences, Engineering, and Medicine.

Robert M. Groves, *Chair*
Panel on the Scope, Components, and Key Characteristics
of a 21st Century Data Infrastructure

Contents

Boxes, Figures, and Tables

BOXES

FIGURES

TABLES

Acronyms and Abbreviations

ACDEB   Advisory Committee on Data for Evidence Building
ACS   American Community Survey
ADC   America's DataHub Consortium
AEAStat   American Economic Association Committee on Statistics

BEA   Bureau of Economic Analysis
BJS   Bureau of Justice Statistics
BLS   U.S. Bureau of Labor Statistics

CDC   Centers for Disease Control and Prevention
CDO   (Federal) Chief Data Officer
CE   Consumer Expenditure Survey
CEP   U.S. Commission on Evidence-Based Policymaking
CIPSEA   Confidential Information Protection and Statistical Efficiency Act
CNSTAT   Committee on National Statistics
CPI   Consumer Price Index
CPS   Current Population Survey
CSDA   Common Statistical Data Architecture
CSPA   Common Statistical Production Architecture

DDI   Data Documentation Initiative
DHS   Department of Homeland Security

EHR   electronic health record

EIA   Energy Information Administration

FCSM   Federal Committee on Statistical Methodology
FFRDC   federally funded research and development center
FGDC   Federal Geographic Data Committee
FISMA   Federal Information Security Management Act
FITARA   Federal Information Technology Acquisition Reform Act
FSRDC   federal statistical research data center

GAO   U.S. Government Accountability Office
GSBPM   Generic Statistical Business Process Model
GSIM   Generic Statistical Information Model

HHS   U.S. Department of Health and Human Services
HIPAA   Health Insurance Portability and Accountability Act

ICPSR   Inter-university Consortium for Political and Social Research
ICSP   Interagency Council on Statistical Policy
IEC   International Electrotechnical Commission
IRB   institutional review board
IRS   Internal Revenue Service
ISO   International Organization for Standardization
IT   information technology

MEPS HC   Medical Expenditure Panel Survey, Household Component
MOUs   memoranda of understanding

NARA   National Archives and Records Administration
NASEM   National Academies of Sciences, Engineering, and Medicine
NIEM   National Information Exchange Model
NIH   National Institutes of Health
NIST   National Institute for Standards and Technology
NRC   National Research Council
NSDS   National Secure Data Service
NSF   National Science Foundation

OECD   Organisation for Economic Co-operation and Development
OMB   U.S. Office of Management and Budget

QCEW   Quarterly Census of Employment and Wages

SAP   Standard Application Process
SBA   Small Business Administration

SDMX	Statistical Data and Metadata eXchange
SHIELD	Stop Hacks and Improve Electronic Data Security Act
SORNs	system of records notices
SSA	Social Security Administration
UNECE	United Nations Economic Commission for Europe
USDA	U.S. Department of Agriculture

Glossary of Select Terms

Data Equity

No common definition exists within the federal government—neither the Equitable Data Working Group in their recent report (The White House, 2022b) nor the U.S. Census Bureau (https://www.census.gov/about/what/data-equity.html) define the term. In this report, data equity "refers to the consideration, through an equity lens, of the ways in which data is collected, analyzed, interpreted, and distributed" (Lee-Ibarra, 2021).

Data Infrastructure

Data assets; the technologies used to discover, access, share, process, use, analyze, manage, store, preserve, protect, and secure those assets; the people, capacity, and expertise needed to manage, use, interpret, and understand data; the guidance, standards, policies, and rules that govern data access, use, and protection; the organizations and entities that manage, oversee, and govern the data infrastructure; and the communities and data subjects whose data is shared and used for statistical purposes and may be impacted by decisions that are made using those data assets.

Equitable Data Working Group

Executive Order 13985, "Advancing Racial Equity and Support for Underserved Communities Through the Federal

Government," issued by President Biden in January 2020, formed the Equitable Data Working Group. It is tasked to identify inadequacies and areas of improvement within federal data and outline a strategy for increasing data available for measuring equity and representing the diversity of the American people and their experiences (The White House, 2021b).

Evidence Act

Also referred to as the "Foundations for Evidence-Based Policymaking Act of 2018." This bill requires agency data to be accessible and requires agencies to plan to develop statistical evidence to support policymaking (U.S. Congress, 2019).

Standard Application Process (SAP)

The federal statistical system is currently developing an SAP for applying for access to confidential data assets. When fully built, the SAP will serve as a "front door" through which to apply for permission to use protected data from any of the 16 federal statistical agencies and units for evidence building (https://ncses.nsf.gov/about/standard-application-process). Testing for the portal will occur in September 2022, with the expectation that the site will be operational by the end of 2022. The current portal is at: https://www.researchdatagov.org/

Summary

Credible statistical information is foundational to the functioning of democratic societies. Just as bridges and highways facilitate the transportation necessary for commerce, statistical information informs decisions by governments, business enterprises, and individuals. The information emerges from a data infrastructure.

Historically, the U.S. national data infrastructure has relied on the operations of the federal statistical system and the data assets that it holds. Throughout the 20th century, federal statistical agencies aggregated survey responses from households and businesses to produce information about the nation and diverse subpopulations. The statistics created from such surveys provide most of what people know about the well-being of society, including health, education, employment, safety, housing, and food security. The surveys also contribute to the infrastructure for empirical social- and economic-sciences research. Research using survey-response data, with strict privacy protections, led to important discoveries about the causes and consequences of important societal challenges and also informed policymakers. Like other infrastructure, people can easily take these essential statistics for granted. Only when they are threatened do people recognize the need to protect them.

Today, paradoxically, national statistics face both grave threats and historic opportunities. Declining survey participation poses a severe threat to the quality of statistical information. Yet, at the same time, the United States has never produced a higher volume of digital data about the activities of individuals and businesses. These data are held in federal, state, and local government agencies, the private sector, and other organizations.

To address these threats and explore the opportunities, the National Academies of Sciences, Engineering, and Medicine appointed a consensus panel to develop a vision for a new data infrastructure for national statistics and social and economic research in the 21st century. This report is the first of three reports funded by the National Science Foundation to explore the many issues surrounding a new data infrastructure. The panel convened a 1.5-day virtual public workshop to seek input from key stakeholders and external experts and to discuss issues surrounding the components and key characteristics of a 21st century national data infrastructure, including governance; the capabilities, techniques, and methods required; and the sharing of data assets (e.g., federal, state, and local government, institutional, and private sector data). This report describes how the country can improve the statistical information so critical to shaping the nation's future, by mobilizing data assets and blending them with existing survey data.

These ideas are compatible with those forwarded in 2017 by the U.S. Commission on Evidence-Based Policymaking (CEP). The report notes that only a subset of CEP's recommendations has been incorporated into law. A new data infrastructure can take advantage of experiences in the five years following the Commission's recommendations to further expand the value and uses of statistical data coordinated from multiple sectors. In the interest of advancing a national data infrastructure, in 2019 the National Academies' Committee on National Statistics formulated the following definition:

> The data infrastructure consists of data assets; the technologies used to discover, access, share, process, use, analyze, manage, store, preserve, protect, and secure those assets; the people, capacity, and expertise needed to manage, use, interpret, and understand data; the guidance, standards, policies, and rules that govern data access, use, and protection; the organizations and entities that manage, oversee, and govern the data infrastructure; and the communities and data subjects whose data is shared and used for statistical purposes and may be impacted by decisions that are made using those data assets.

A new data infrastructure can mobilize the nation's relevant data assets by combining data across sectors, to improve existing statistical products, create new ones, and strengthen research capabilities. Modern technologies permitting secure access to multiple datasets along with new computational methods can allow the blending of data for more timely, granular, and accurate statistics. Further, this blending can involve enhanced privacy protections for data subjects and holders. New privacy-enhancing tools can minimize threats to individuals. However, the mere availability of new data assets and technologies to improve the nation's statistical information and research base is not enough—the United States needs a vision for new partnerships across data holders to take advantage of a new data infrastructure.

The United States needs a new 21st century national data infrastructure that blends data from multiple sources to improve the quality, timeliness, granularity, and usefulness of national statistics, facilitates more rigorous social and economic research, and supports evidence-based policymaking and program evaluations. (Conclusion 2-1)

In the panel's view, a new data infrastructure should allow statistical agencies and other approved users (federal, state, tribal, territory, and local government employees and researchers) to use the country's data assets for purposes of the common good. These assets include data from federal statistical, program, and administrative agencies; state, tribal, territory, and local governments; private sector companies; nonprofits and academic institutions; and crowdsourcing and citizen science operations. Innovative pilot projects now offer convincing proof of the potential value to be gained from more effective use of the nation's data resources.

This report is the first in a series intended to help build a vision for a new data infrastructure for the common good. This report describes the need for a new national data infrastructure, presents an initial vision, and describes expected outcomes and key attributes of a new national data infrastructure. The report also discusses the implications of blending data from multiple sources as well as the organizational implications of cross-sector data access and use. The report concludes by identifying short- and medium-term activities that facilitate progress toward the full vision. This report does not examine the logical, physical, or technical architecture for a new infrastructure or specific technical capabilities related to data formats or metadata, encryption or security protocols, access controls, or organizational functions and responsibilities. Future reports will explore associated topics in greater depth, including case studies and implications of blending multiple sources, data equity, and other relevant data infrastructure issues, challenges, and opportunities identified during each panel's deliberations. The existing data ecosystem is evolving rapidly and the goal of each subsequent report is to respond to these changes and focus on the specific issues, opportunities, and challenges deemed most relevant to implementing and operationalizing the different components of a new data infrastructure.

ATTRIBUTES OF THE VISION

The panel identified seven key attributes of a new data infrastructure (see Box S-1). These attributes are detailed in the sections that follow, along with associated short-term actions that should be undertaken to begin

---

BOX S-1
Seven Attributes of a 21st Century
National Data Infrastructure Vision

1. Safeguards and advanced privacy-enhancing practices to minimize possible individual harm.
2. Statistical uses <u>only</u>, for common-good information, with statistical aggregates freely shared with all.
3. Mobilization of relevant digital data assets, blended in statistical aggregates to providing benefits to data holders, with societal benefits proportionate to possible costs and risks.
4. Reformed legal authorities protecting all parties' interests.
5. Governance framework and standards effectively supporting operations.
6. Transparency to the public regarding analytical operations using the infrastructure.
7. State-of-the-art practices for access, statistical, coordination, and computational activities; continuously improved to efficiently create increasingly secure and useful information.

SOURCE: Panel generated.

---

building a 21st century national data infrastructure for social and economic data, and the research the infrastructure could facilitate.

Safeguards and Advanced Privacy-Enhancing Practices to Minimize Possible Individual Harm

The panel notes that the social benefits of statistical information need not come at the price of increased threats to individuals' privacy and confidentiality; the interests and rights of data subjects must be respected. In the panel's view, any harm to individuals from building and operating a new data infrastructure should be minimized. Novel technologies and strong regulations can be applied to strengthen safeguards for individuals. Laws, regulations, and practices should employ the most current and effective tools to protect the privacy of individuals. Furthermore, the blending of data involves little new data collection; instead, existing data will be used more efficiently. With harm minimized and benefits increased by improved statistical information, society will be better served.

It is ethically necessary and technically possible to preserve privacy and fulfill confidentiality pledges regarding data while simultaneously expanding the statistical uses of diverse data sources. (Conclusion 3-1)

Short-Term Actions

1. Establish mechanisms to engage stakeholders (including data subjects, data holders, and other responsible organizations) regarding data safeguard prerequisites for building trust.
2. Develop a strategy to ensure key data safeguards are communicated effectively and transparently.
3. Establish technical specifications of privacy-preserving and confidentiality-protecting designs.

Statistical Uses Only, for Common-Good Information, with Statistical Aggregates Freely Shared with All

In the panel's vision, data-infrastructure resources produce nonidentifiable aggregates, estimates, and statistics, to use statistical aggregation to create useful information for society and decisionmakers without harming individuals. Data-infrastructure operations and decisions are consistent with professional principles and practices, meet ethical standards, are conducted by organizations free of political interference, and are managed to ensure privacy and security.[1] Data cannot be used for the enforcement of laws or regulations affecting any individual data subject.

Short-Term Actions

1. Use pilots to promote a wider understanding of "statistical uses."
2. Convene stakeholders to determine how to best describe new statistical products and distinguish them from privacy-threatening initiatives.
3. Monitor outcomes of the new Standard Application Process (SAP) for research use of shared data to demonstrate value.
4. Launch a communication campaign about the value of research as a "statistical use" of data.

Mobilization of Relevant Digital Data Assets, Blended in Statistical Aggregates to Provide Benefits to Data Holders, with Societal Benefits Proportionate to Possible Costs and Risks

In the panel's vision, a new data infrastructure should have access to relevant, existing, digital assets for the creation of essential aggregates.

---

[1]In this chapter and throughout the report, the term "professionalism" in compiling national statistics—either within the existing federal statistical system or the new data infrastructure—is based on authoritative information presented by the National Academies of Sciences, Engineering, and Medicine (2021).

The infrastructure should mobilize and leverage data assets across various sectors. Each data asset has strengths and weaknesses; counterbalancing features by blending data sources results in improved information.

> Data from federal, state, tribal, territory, and local governments; the private sector; nonprofits and academic institutions; and crowdsourced and citizen-science data holders are crucial components of a 21st century national data infrastructure. (Conclusion 4-1)

In the panel's vision, a new data infrastructure will include a wider variety of data holders, data subjects, data seekers, and data users than in the past. To achieve the support of all involved parties, demonstrating the benefits of expanded data sharing and blending is critical.

> Data sharing is incentivized when all data holders enjoy tangible benefits valuable to their missions, and when societal benefits are proportionate to possible costs and risks. (Conclusion 3-2)

Short-Term Actions

1. Seek researcher input regarding SAP implementation as an access tool.
2. Monitor activities of the Interagency Council on Statistical Policy working group on private sector data.
3. Monitor "data-connecting" pilots collecting data at the data holder's site.
4. Publish criteria for prioritizing new data assets.
5. Convene a group to evaluate methods for documenting and, possibly, quantifying benefits and costs.
6. Identify blended statistics generated by statistical agencies; document and, possibly, quantify benefits and costs.
7. Monitor pilot projects for blended federal/state/local data.
8. Consider the feasibility and means of covering some data-holder costs associated with data sharing.

Reformed Legal Authorities Protecting All Parties' Interests

Under the Foundations for Evidence-Based Policymaking Act of 2018 (hereafter, Evidence Act), federal statistical agencies have the right to use federal program data for statistical uses only, unless directly prohibited by law. However, many laws and regulations do prohibit federal statistical agencies from using existing data for statistical purposes. In the panel's vision of a 21st century national data infrastructure, it is assumed that the legislative and regulatory recommendations stemming from the Evidence Act will be initiated, but more work is needed to bolster data safeguards and broaden data access.

Legal and regulatory changes are necessary to achieve the full promise of a 21st century national data infrastructure. (Conclusion 3-3)

Short-Term Actions

1. Legislation establishing the design, authorities, and funding for the National Secure Data Service (NSDS).[2]
2. Implement Evidence Act regulations and rule-making.
3. Identify legislation/regulatory priorities regarding CEP state-related recommendations.
4. Develop a data synchronization bill[3] legislative strategy.
5. Identify legal options that would incentivize data holders to share data.

Governance Framework and Standards Effectively Supporting Operations

In the panel's opinion, legal reforms enabling a new data infrastructure must be accompanied by a set of practices and policies consistent with the spirit of the law. Such a data-governance framework includes guiding principles, authorities, structures, and directives for the infrastructure. Data governance involves active stakeholder engagement, oversight protocols, open and transparent communications, and accountability. Standards in data definitions and access protocols are critical to providing interoperability across partners essential to a new data infrastructure. In addition, professional staff throughout the infrastructure will require an environment that supports interoperability and provides them with modern skills and technology.

Effective data governance is critical and should be inclusive and accountable; governance policies and standards facilitating interoperability include key stakeholders and oversight bodies. (Conclusion 3-4)

---

[2]The CHIPS and Science Act (P.L. 117-167) was signed into law on August 9th, 2022. It allocates funding for an unnamed demonstration project to inform establishment of NSDS.

[3]Such legislation would revise Internal Revenue Service regulations to allow the U.S. Census Bureau to share limited business tax data with the Bureau of Labor Statistics and the Bureau of Economic Analysis.

Short-Term Actions

1. Convene potential data-holding organizations.
2. Document current practices in data access.
3. Catalog current data platforms of potential data-sharing organizations.
4. Document current methods of data curation, protection, and preservation.
5. Document existing metadata practices.
6. Identify priorities for standards development.
7. Draft data-sharing guidelines.

Transparency to the Public Regarding Analytical Operations Using the Infrastructure

In the panel's opinion, at any time, the public, data holders, and data subjects should be able to understand how their data are used, by whom, for what purposes, and to what societal benefit. Transparency is a prerequisite for accountability, enabling the public to express concerns, seek redress, and oversee compliance with a new data infrastructure's stated mission. Transparency is also a prerequisite for public trust. Trust and transparent procedures will enhance the credibility of the statistical information produced through a new data infrastructure.

Trust in a new data infrastructure requires transparency of operations and accountability of the operators, with ongoing engagement of stakeholders. (Conclusion 3-5)

Short-Term Actions

1. Identify communication priorities regarding transparency.
2. Sponsor public discussion regarding alternative oversight structures to achieve transparency.
3. Engage stakeholders to evaluate alternative approaches.

State-of-the-Art Practices for Access, Statistical, Coordination, and Computational Activities; Continuously Improved to Efficiently Create Increasingly Secure and Useful Information

The panel predicts that the technical aspects of a new data infrastructure will be highly dynamic. New developments in remote access, cybersecurity, cryptography, and computational approaches are constantly emerging. Thus, in the panel's view, operations within a new data infrastructure must continually innovate and improve. On the computational and statistical side, the infrastructure must be able to blend data for more insightful research and statistical products. The acquisition, access, and use of diverse data assets held by multiple organizations in various sectors will likely involve new partners with divergent experiences and expertise. The dynamic nature of all these features demands continuous refreshing of the skill mix of the infrastructure's operational staff.

The operations of a new data infrastructure would benefit from the inclusion of continually evolving practices, methods, technologies, and skills, to ethically leverage new technologies and advanced methods. (Conclusion 3-6)

Short-Term Actions

1. Exchange knowledge about needed staff skillsets to support new operations of infrastructure.
2. Build communities of practice to catalyze the technical skills base.
3. Develop a professional culture within pilot projects for data protection.
4. Develop organizational procedures for continuous updating of tools and practices.

Many Options for Supporting a New Data Infrastructure

Alternative ideas have been promulgated for organizing statistical operations within a new data infrastructure. The key new entity (or set of entities) needed is not a data warehouse, but rather a computational resource for linking data files in diverse ways, to produce blended statistics. The panel foresees several potential organizational models for this new entity: within the federal government, outside the federal government, or as a new public-private partnership. To identify the best option, the panel suggests the initiation of a widespread dialogue involving the many stakeholders of a new data infrastructure.

Short-Term Actions

1. Monitor America's DataHub Consortium capabilities for collaborative research partnerships and data sharing.
2. Clarify data infrastructure roles and responsibilities.
3. Identify NSDS-provided services and capabilities.
4. Clarify federal statistical research data center services and capabilities.

5. Sponsor bipartisan, multisector dialogue on how best to govern private sector data use for national statistical purposes.
6. Expand voluntary private sector data sharing for statistical uses.

Building a New Data Infrastructure

This report comes at a time of unusual change. Numerous research and statistical agency initiatives are blending data from multiple sources, and these initiatives will undoubtedly inform future activities, including social and economic research. While some new laws and regulations have been enacted, obstacles remain, and more legislative work needs to be done. Some initial building blocks of a new data infrastructure are under construction but lack a coordinated vision. For example, CEP proposed NSDS to produce statistical information for evidence-building by temporarily accessing multiple federal programs and statistical data assets and blending them as needed. The panel sees the value of NSDS for informing the public about the well-being of the economy and society, and for advising future data-blending entities.

There are many ways to achieve the vision of a 21st century national data infrastructure, and it is too early to identify each step necessary to achieve that vision. The panel suggests leveraging the many ongoing initiatives, both domestically and internationally, looking for early examples of success. This will require forging new partnerships with data holders, key data-infrastructure entities, and interested stakeholders. In addition to the short-term activities associated with each of the seven key attributes and potential organizational models mentioned above, the panel identified a set of medium-term activities (Table 5-1) that could be performed to discern the best ways for the United States to proceed toward the panel's full vision.

> In building a 21st century national data infrastructure, early success may come first from integrating data that are relatively easily available, demonstrating the utility of improved statistical information of national importance, and constructing effective partnerships for necessary legal change. (**Conclusion 5-1**)

The United States is capable of building a new national data infrastructure. If such an infrastructure is designed appropriately, the American public and decisionmakers could enjoy more timely, granular, and accurate information about the country's employment, housing, income, education, health, safety, transportation, and food security.

1

Introduction

Informed decisions about every aspect of life—career and job seeking, housing, public health, energy, transportation, food supplies, crime prevention, commerce, and any other area one can think of—rely on credible, accurate, objective, and relevant data. Historically, countries have responded to this need by assigning central governments the responsibility for producing statistics (Davies et al., 2019). These data provide the foundation for basic and applied social-, behavioral-, and economic-sciences research, which helps research, policy-analysis, and program-evaluation communities understand and make informed decisions regarding the economy and society. A country's data infrastructure is analogous to the bridges and highways that make up the physical transportation infrastructure necessary for commerce. Like other types of infrastructure, these essential statistics can easily be taken for granted until they fail to meet the needs of individuals or society in some way.

This report is the first in a series intended to help build a vision for a new data infrastructure for the common good. This report describes the need for a new national data infrastructure, presents an initial vision, and describes the expected outcomes and key attributes of such an infrastructure. The report also discusses the implications of blending data from multiple sources as well as the organizational implications of cross-sector data access and use. The report concludes by identifying short- and medium-term activities to facilitate progress toward the full vision. Future reports will explore associated topics in greater depth, including case studies and implications of blending multiple sources, data equity, and other data infrastructure-related challenges and opportunities.

BACKGROUND

Several experts and organizations, including the U.S. Commission on Evidence-Based Policymaking (CEP), have recognized threats to the current data infrastructure, the necessity of strengthening that infrastructure, and the opportunities for doing so. In recent years, the Committee on National Statistics (CNSTAT), a standing board of the National Academies of Sciences, Engineering, and Medicine, has initiated and overseen work that could enhance federal statistics by blending and integrating a variety of administrative and other data sources (the National Academies of Sciences, Engineering, and Medicine, 2017a,b). These studies explored the growing concern that participation in federal sample-survey data collections, the archetypal method of measurement, has continually decreased over the past 15, or more, years (e.g., U.S. Bureau of Labor Statistics, 2022). If participation is dominated by a particular subgroup of respondents low-response-rate surveys have an increased risk of biased statistics (Czajka and Beyler, 2016; Groves and Peytcheva, 2008). Moreover, uneven spatial patterns of responses can give data from certain locations greater uncertainty, potentially resulting in the misallocation of critical federal resources.

The National Academies' studies highlighted the nearly singular reliance on survey data for federal statistics, noting that "surveys and censuses are currently the principal means of collecting federal statistics. The Census Bureau alone conducts more than 130 economic and demographic surveys every year" (the National Academies, 2017b, p. 22). As survey response rates have decreased, alternative data sources (transactional, geospatial, scanner, and sensor) have become increasingly available to blend with other sources, and the National Academies' reports also offered guidance to federal agencies regarding technical solutions for working with alternative data sources.

Similarly, CEP reported that "household survey data collection programs, including key U.S. Census Bureau programs, are finding it more difficult to obtain accurate income data from the survey population" (Commission on Evidence-Based Policymaking, 2017, p. 5). In the same report, CEP called for a space in which data from multiple sources could be blended, while protecting privacy and confidentiality:

> The Congress and the President should enact legislation establishing the National Secure Data Service (NSDS) to facilitate data access for evidence building while ensuring transparency and privacy. The NSDS should model best practices for secure record linkage and drive the implementation of innovative privacy-enhancing technologies (Commission on Evidence-Based Policymaking, 2017, p. 5).

To build on these efforts, CNSTAT has been considering several issues, including how to advance the vision of NSDS, how the statistical system should adapt to an increasingly digitized world, and how to build a vision for a future data infrastructure. To complement the efforts of the Foundations for Evidence-Based Policymaking Act of 2018 to implement CEP's recommendations, CNSTAT focused on data sources not currently within the scope of other efforts, such as state, tribal, territorial, and local government data, as well as private sector data. In 2019, CNSTAT formulated the following definition of data infrastructure to guide future work:[1]

> The data infrastructure consists of data assets; the technologies used to discover, access, share, process, use, analyze, manage, store, preserve, protect, and secure those assets; the people, capacity, and expertise needed to manage, use, interpret, and understand data; the guidance, standards, policies, and rules that govern data access, use, and protection; the organizations and entities that manage, oversee, and govern the data infrastructure; and the communities and data subjects whose data is shared and used for statistical purposes and may be impacted by decisions that are made using those data assets.

This report is the first of three targeted consensus reports by separate panels exploring specific aspects of a 21st century national data infrastructure. Each consensus panel will convene a public workshop as its primary vehicle for external fact-gathering. Cumulatively, the three panels and their respective reports are intended to contribute to a vision for a 21st century national data infrastructure for federal statistics that will support social and economic research into the future.[2] The project, overseen by CNSTAT, is funded by the National Science Foundation. The project's statement of task can be seen in Box 1-1. The tasks of this panel—the Panel on the Scope, Components, and Key Characteristics of a 21st Century Data Infrastructure—are outlined in this report, Report 1.

The first paragraph in Box 1-1 bears particular relevance. The vision outlined in this and subsequent reports is for a *new* data infrastructure. Reports 2 and 3 will explore aspects of this vision including case studies and implications of blending multiple data sources; data equity; and other relevant data infrastructure issues, challenges, and opportunities that are identified during each panel's deliberations. The existing data ecosystem is evolving rapidly, and the goal of Report 3 is to respond

---

[1]This definition was created for internal use and was presented at the 2020 CNSTAT Retreat based on a paper (entitled "A Suggested Framework for Discussion") by Tom Mesenbourg.

[2]For more information, see: https://www.nationalacademies.org/our-work/toward-a-vision-for-a-new-data-infrastructure-for-federal-statistics-and-social-and-economic-research-in-the-21st-century

BOX 1-1
Statement of Task

The National Academies of Sciences, Engineering, and Medicine will appoint an ad hoc committee to produce three complementary reports on topics that will help guide the development of a vision for a new data infrastructure for federal statistics and social and economic research in the 21st century. The topics the committee will explore include the following:

Report 1: The components and key characteristics of a 21st Century Data Infrastructure including:
- **The challenges and opportunities related to data infrastructure governance;**
- **The skills, capabilities, techniques, and methods required by the new data infrastructure; and**
- **Issues related to sharing non-traditional data assets, including state and local government, institutional, private sector, and sensor data;**

Report 2: The implications of using multiple data sources for major survey programs, including:
- Addressing changes in measurement with new data sources;
- Approaches for linking alternative data sources to universe frames to assess and enhance representativeness; and
- Implications of new data sources for population subgroup coverage, and life course longitudinal data;

Report 3: Approaches for data governance and protecting privacy. Formerly titled: The technology, tools, and capabilities needed for data sharing, use, and analysis, including:
- Alternative approaches and techniques for protecting privacy and confidentiality;
- Alternative sustainable organizational models for data sharing; and
- Approaches to ensure transparency of the datasets, the use of the data, as well as the resulting products.

The committee for each report will convene a 1.5 day virtual public workshop for each topic to seek input from key stakeholders and external experts relevant to the specific charge. Each committee will issue a report that summarizes the committee's findings and conclusions from the workshop and other information gathered relevant to the charge, as appropriate. These reports will help inform a vision for a new data infrastructure and will not include recommendations. The three reports will follow institutional guidelines and be subject to the National Academies review procedures prior to release.

to these changes and focus on technical issues deemed most relevant to implementing and operationalizing various components of a potential new data infrastructure.

INTERPRETATION OF THE CHARGE

The panel's fundamental focus was improving federal statistics, with the recognition that increasing the availability and utility of all relevant data could not only improve said statistics but also support research and evidence-building for the public good. As a result, in formulating its vision, the panel looked beyond federally controlled and directed data assets as specified in the Evidence Act.

The panel's vision for a new data infrastructure includes all relevant data assets held by federal, state, tribal, territory, and local governments; the private sector; nonprofit and academic institutions; as well as crowd-sourced and citizen-science organizations. Besides federal statistical and administrative data assets, process-related, sensor/monitoring, and other data assets could be included if they are consistent with data infrastructure purposes. While the scope of potential data assets is expansive, this report focuses on data assets that can improve social and economic statistics and research. Consequently, this report does not examine issues related to using sensor data. Nevertheless, the panel foresees the possible integration of sensor data into national statistics once techniques exist to accurately assess their fitness for use and to address important security and privacy issues (U.S. Government Accountability Office, 2020). Subsequent workshops may focus on sensor, monitor, process, and other alternative data assets.

The panel examined evidence to inform key components and characteristics of a new data infrastructure and determined that challenges and opportunities to its creation include not only issues of data infrastructure governance but also other important considerations that warrant individual attention. These attributes (as the panel labeled them) include safeguards for data subjects and holders, legal and regulatory issues that directly impact the ability of infrastructure participants to share data, and transparency of infrastructure processes and practices. These attributes comprise part of the broader ecosystem in which a new data infrastructure would operate.

This report does not examine the logical, physical, or technical architecture of new infrastructure, nor does it describe specific technical capabilities related to data formats or metadata, encryption or security protocols, access controls, or organizational functions and responsibilities. The panel focused on a high-level vision, identifying the components and key characteristics of a 21st century national data infrastructure, including governance; the required capabilities, techniques, and methods; and the data assets that could be shared. This report describes how the United States can improve the statistical information so critical to shaping the nation's future, by mobilizing data assets and blending them with existing survey data. Future work should examine whether new data infrastructures should be designed in a federated manner or through a centralized data intermediary.

The composition of the panel reflects a focus on social and economic research as an integral part of a new data infrastructure. Note that the physical or natural sciences are not mentioned in the charge. While research techniques from computer science and engineering, for example, are commonly deployed in the social sciences, primary data from the physical and natural sciences are rarely used in the creation of national statistics describing the social and economic status of the United States.

EVIDENCE BASE FOR REPORT

In executing its charge, the panel sought evidence from wide and disparate sources, including groups of experts that previously identified obstacles to the blending of data to improve national statistics. In addition to CEP and the 2017 National Academies' reports mentioned above, the panel closely followed the Advisory Committee on Data for Evidence Building (ACDEB), which was founded based on a recommendation in the CEP report (Commission on Evidence-Based Policymaking, 2017). ACDEB is tasked with "assisting the Director of the Office of Management and Budget on issues of access to data and providing recommendations on how to facilitate data sharing, data linkage, and privacy-enhancing techniques" (U.S. Department of Commerce, 2022). Similar to the CEP report, ACDEB is not actively researching the utility of blending private sector data with data assets from the federal statistical system.

The panel also examined peer-reviewed papers, white papers, and United States (as well as non-U.S.) government policies and planning documents, but found no individuals or groups pursuing a new national data infrastructure integrating multiple sources as envisioned by the panel.[3] The panel aims to advise the organization of these data at a national scale, to improve national statistics. Combining these data will only be possible within a suitable legal, governance, and organizational structure that delineates services, responsibilities, and access procedures while improving current privacy and confidentiality protections. Thus, the panel describes current impediments and considers the appropriate attributes that will enable a successful transformation to a new data infrastructure.

---

[3]Two earlier, successful government-led initiatives to integrate data are the Longitudinal Employer-Household Dynamics program (https://lehd.ces.census.gov/) and the Criminal Justice Administrative Records System (https://cjars.isr.umich.edu/). These initiatives fulfilled important sectoral goals rather than demonstrating a federal statistical system approach.

To address gaps in the literature and to provide a forum for public comment, the panel convened two public workshops in December 2021 (hereafter, referred to as "the workshops"). The workshops were organized into five sessions:

1. Data Infrastructure Initiatives—Description and Discussion;
2. Private Sector Data Uses for National Statistical Purposes—International Perspectives;
3. Federal Statistical Agencies Uses of Private Sector Transaction Data;
4. Federal Statistical Agencies' and Nonprofits' Use of Private Sector Health Data; and
5. Perspectives on Using Private Sector Data for Official Statistics and Research.

The utility of private sector data to improve national statistics was a focus of most sessions, as these data have not been included in other efforts (see Appendix B for complete workshop agendas). Importantly, the panel asked participants to describe the impediments they confronted while attempting to blend alternative (usually private sector) data sources to improve national statistics. Employees from statistical agencies in the United States and Europe, researchers, and private sector representatives shared lessons learned from these activities, including legal and technical constraints and contractual issues related to acquiring and working with private sector data. Their collective contributions were influential in the panel's deliberations.

The absence of workshop sessions on state, tribal, territorial, and local data does not mean these data are unimportant; rather, in the panel's opinion, previous reports and the work of ACDEB—with a sizable number of members routinely working with these data—can provide the guidance that the panel lacked either the time or expertise to address.[4] As noted throughout this report, state, tribal, territorial, and local data could vastly improve the country's knowledge of itself, including better measurements within geographical locations or among subgroups of interest.

REPORT STRUCTURE

As noted in Box 1-1, this report offers conclusions on the scope, components, and key characteristics of a 21st century national data infrastructure and the vital role of the federal statistical system in such an infrastructure.

---

[4] Advisory Committee on Data for Evidence Building (2021) identifies current obstacles to integrating state and local data into the production of national statistics.

Chapter 2 describes why the United States needs a new data infrastructure. It details current modernization efforts, opportunities afforded by the explosion of digital data produced inside and outside of government, and ongoing government-led initiatives to repair weaknesses in national statistics using alternative data sources. The chapter highlights reports that recommend the use of blended data, and it discusses recent congressional efforts, which are necessary but insufficient, to expand data access and use.

Chapter 3 describes a vision for a new data infrastructure, the expected outcomes, and the seven key attributes of that infrastructure. Each of the seven attributes is discussed in detail, with a description of the current challenges involved and the changes necessary to attain each attribute.

Chapter 4 describes the diverse data assets that can be combined for statistical purposes; the criteria that govern data acquisition, access, and use; the implications of blended data for the format of a new data infrastructure; and the associated privacy and ethical challenges. The chapter ends with a consideration of various organizational structures that may facilitate cross-sector data access and use.

Chapters 1–4 set the stage for the final chapter. In this time of innovation and change, many components of a new data infrastructure could be achieved in multiple ways. Rather than identifying sequential steps for implementing a new data infrastructure, the panel identifies short- and medium-term tasks that contribute to the implementation of the panel's full vision. These tasks involve engaging with key stakeholders to inform appropriate next steps and to gain stakeholder support for a new data infrastructure.

2

The United States Needs a
New National Data Infrastructure

BACKGROUND

An informed citizenry is foundational to a modern democracy. Information about the welfare of the population—its health and safety, educational achievement, occupational skill distribution, employment status, wealth, housing status, and hundreds of other attributes—guides the assessment of a country's well-being. Information about the status of the economy similarly prompts judgment: Are firms growing? Are they investing in the future? Are they planning new ventures? Are new startups prevalent? What is the state and trend of economic inequality? Are federal resources allocated to subpopulations fairly and according to societal priorities, and are they distributed to locations where they are most needed? To assess current conditions as well as the performance of elected officials and the policies they pursue, citizens of democracies require authoritative and trustworthy statistics. The absence of such facts can leave citizens vulnerable to misinformation and disinformation—a threat to democracy itself.

In all democracies throughout the world, central governments have the responsibility of collecting data and making statistical information widely available to the populace. Credibility is a key attribute of information distributed from the government to the public. To achieve credibility, a set of essential principles, policies, and procedures insulates the collection of such statistical information from political interference. In some countries, a central bureau of statistics is protected by laws that grant legal independence to the methods and inquiries of statistical bureaus (e.g., The Statistics

Act passed by the Parliament of Canada in 1918).[1] Such laws distinguish between administrative uses of data, in which individual-level data can be used for purposes such as determining program eligibility, and statistical uses of data, which produce aggregate estimates about populations. In the United States, the Confidential Information Protection and Statistical Efficiency Act of 2002 (U.S. Congress, 2002b) and other statutes ensure that data provided by respondents to federal statistical agencies for statistical purposes are confidential.

Government statistical agencies often articulate a set of principles, practices, and standards to ensure the trustworthiness and credibility of government statistics. For example, the seventh edition of *Principles and Practices for a Federal Statistical Agency* identifies "credibility among data users and stakeholders" and "independence from political and other undue external influence" as two of five well-established and fundamental principles (National Academies of Sciences, Engineering, and Medicine, 2021, pp. 5–6).

To enhance trust, laws prohibit statistical agencies from using data for enforcement purposes or intervening in the activities of individuals or businesses. Instead, statistical uses of data typically describe large populations and are constructed using aggregates of individual data. Statistical information should be relevant to policymakers but not espouse specific policy recommendations. Information should be timely and useful to decision-makers, while also providing an accurate description of the country's full population. Much statistical information tracks change over time for some feature or attribute of the country; hence, information should be consistent over time and location. Measurements upon which statistical information is based should accurately assess the concepts in question, that is, measurements should be fit for use. Together, these practices ensure the credibility of government statistics.

Historically, statistical agencies of central governments designed their own *de novo* measurement systems (e.g., for determining employment status). Registers listing each member of a given target population identify the persons or organizations eligible to be measured. Statistical agencies carefully construct these sampling frames to include all eligible members of a given target population—a hallmark of modern government statistics. Statistical sampling techniques identify a subset of the eligible members that represent the full population. Data collection typically involves self-administered questionnaires or interviews in every sampled unit. Statistical theories prescribe that unbiased statistics are produced when each sampled member of the population is measured. Consequently, statistical agencies expend great effort to contact, gain cooperation, and measure sampled units.

---

[1] See: https://laws-lois.justice.gc.ca/eng/acts/S-19/FullText.html

United States government statistical agencies produce more than just statistical information for monitoring the status of the country's society and economy. The data assets of these agencies also create a research infrastructure for the empirical social and economic sciences and are used by government, academic, and nonacademic research organizations. The research uses of data, with the continuous exercise of strict privacy protections, have generated important discoveries that have directly influenced society's awareness and understanding of key issues and informed policymakers' proposals and programs. These include new insights about job creation and destruction, social mobility, job-to-job flows, housing affordability, the gig economy, health and education outcomes, morbidity and mortality, welfare and the wellbeing of children, crime and crime victimization, employer and household dynamics, and much more. Research findings also help the public separate fact from fiction. This research infrastructure, supported by statistical-agency data assets, generates essential shared knowledge about the country.

The U.S. federal statistical system has been the primary producer of statistics and an important research facilitator, but the nation lacks the data infrastructure needed to meet the demands of the 21st century.

MOTIVATION

Recent innovations in computer science and data analytics, combined with an explosion of available digital data, have set the stage for a re-examination of the infrastructure that produces the nation's statistics and supports vital social and economic research. The country's emerging data assets, growing expertise in accessing high-dimensional data, and the pressing need to address evolving societal threats (e.g., pandemics, social injustice, and climate change) call for envisioning a new data infrastructure that produces more timely, granular, and relevant statistical information.

A new data infrastructure will mobilize the nation's relevant data assets by accessing data across sectors, to improve existing statistical products and create new ones—all in scientifically sound ways that incorporate enhanced privacy protections for data subjects and holders. Over time, statistical agencies have improved individual products by expanding their collections, and, occasionally, using administrative records and private sector data. Unfortunately, these remain exceptions, not the rule. The availability of new data assets and technologies is not enough—in the panel's opinion, the United States should use new data assets and technologies within a coordinated, new, national data infrastructure, to meet the information and research needs of the 21st century.

In the panel's judgment, the time is right to develop such a reformed, enriched national data infrastructure. Moreover, the federal statistical system faces myriad and worsening challenges that demand building a new data infrastructure now, not later. The following sections will describe the state of the existing federal statistical system, the challenges it faces, and the impetus for change.

Producing National Statistics: Declining Response Rates and Increased Costs

In the panel's opinion, U.S. statistical agencies' reliance on sample-survey data and census data is unsustainable. The statistical theories that underlie these methods *do* offer strong support for measuring a statistical sample of a population and show that such methods can produce high-quality descriptions of the full population, all while protecting confidentiality. In the 20th century, this approach served the world well (e.g., Rao and Prasad, 1986; Biemer, 2010).

However, inferences based on sample surveys require full measurement of the sample drawn. If some sample units are not measured, the theories require further assumptions that contemporary surveys cannot satisfy. This basic requirement of survey sampling has led to expensive efforts by government statistical agencies to increase participation and response rates. Unfortunately, most of these efforts have failed, regardless of investment, leading to incomplete measurement and increasing the risk of inaccuracies in statistical information. Table 2-1 shows the declining response rates for several important household surveys. It should be noted that the overall response rate is generally unrelated to the separate problem of nonresponse bias, in which only a nonrepresentative group of sample members participate (e.g., Czajka and Beyler, 2016). In a telling example, the pandemic exacerbated these declines in participation and led the U.S. Census Bureau to suspend the release of the 2020 one-year American Community Survey (ACS) estimates (U.S. Census Bureau, 2021a) and, for the first time, delay the release of the five-year ACS products (Bahrampour, 2021). Experimental estimates for 2020 were released on November 30, 2021, but the estimates are not comparable with prior one-year estimates (U.S. Census Bureau, 2021b, 2021c).

The increasing costs of obtaining participation and flat or declining budgets have led to the elimination, or threat of elimination, of multiple important programs and surveys (Box 2-1). For example, in 1996, the National Vital Statistics System, part of the National Center for Health Statistics, suspended the collection of detailed national records-based data on marriages and divorces (Centers for Disease Control and Prevention, 2022). In 2008, after publishing fourth-quarter 2007 estimates, the U.S. Census Bureau terminated its quarterly survey measuring residential alterations, improvements, and repairs (U.S. Census Bureau, 2007). In the absence of official

TABLE 2-1 Selected Household Survey Response Rates

Survey Data	CPS[a]	CPI Housing[b]	CE Interview[c]	MEPS HC[d]	ACS-Annual
Jan 2012	90.4	66.2	71.3	61.3 (overall)	97.3 (weighted)
Jan 2014	89.5	70.8	67.0	52.8	96.7
Jan 2016	86.7	68.2	63.7	51.0	94.7
Jan 2018	84.6	65.4	58.6	46.8	92.0
Jan 2019	83.1	63.3	57.6	46.0	86.0
Jan 2020	81.7	63.9	53.2	NA	71.2
Jan 2021	78.2	52.4	43.7	NA	NA
Jan 2022	73.3	52.6	NA		

SOURCE: Response rates were found on the websites of the U.S. Bureau of Labor Statistics (for CPS, CPI Housing, and CE Interview columns, see https://www.bls.gov/osmr/response-rates/household-survey-response-rates.htm), the Agency for Healthcare Research and Quality (for MEPS HC column, see https://meps.ahrq.gov/mepsweb/survey_comp/hc_response_rate.jsp), and U.S. Census Bureau (for ACS-Annual column, see https://www.census.gov/acs/www/methodology/sample-size-and-data-quality/response-rates/).
[a]Current Population Survey, U.S. Census Bureau.
[b]Consumer Price Index Housing Survey, U.S. Bureau of Labor Statistics.
[c]Consumer Expenditure Survey, U.S. Bureau of Labor Statistics.
[d]Medical Expenditure Panel Survey, Household Component, Agency for Healthcare Research and Quality.

BOX 2-1
Terminated and Threatened Statistical Programs

- National detailed records-based statistics on marriages and divorces dropped from the National Vital Statistics System in 1996.
- U.S. Census Bureau quarterly Survey of Residential Alterations and Repairs terminated in 2008.
- U.S. Bureau of Labor Statistics Mass Layoff Statistics Program eliminated due to fiscal year (FY) 2013 budget sequestration.
- U.S. Census Bureau's Information and Communication Technology Survey eliminated as a result of FY 2013 sequestration.
- American Community Survey suspended 2020 one-year estimates (produced experimental estimates) and delayed five-year products—announced November 2021.

SOURCE: Panel generated.

statistics, private sector estimates of the size of the home-improvement marketplace vary widely. For 2020, private sector estimates ranged from $150 billion (Statista, 2022) to $325–333 billion (Joint Center for Housing Studies, 2020). The elimination of the U.S. Bureau of Labor Statistics (BLS) Mass Layoff Statistics program, a BLS-state cooperative program, resulted in the loss of a standardized approach across states to identify, describe, and track the effects of major job losses (U.S. Bureau of Labor Statistics, n.d.). With the loss of the Information & Communication Technology Survey, there are no longer official annual estimates of information, communication, and technology equipment or software purchases—a huge and growing market (Market Research Store, 2021). According to a report commissioned by the Census Project, a nonpartisan advocacy group, the future of the ACS is threatened (Hoeksema et al., 2022). Experts argued that the ACS, a survey central to the nation's data infrastructure, needs an additional $100–300 million in funding to address current limitations and introduce much-needed enhancements. Other programs, such as the Survey of Income and Program Participation, have lost funding, regained funding, experienced periodic funding shortfalls in the late 1980s, and were later redesigned and continue to this day (U.S. Census Bureau, 2021d).

Declining response rates,[2] increasing collection costs, program reductions, and government continuing resolutions that freeze funding at the prior-year level and increase agency uncertainty, combined with the inability of federal statistical agency budgets to satisfy the growing demand for more timely and granular information, have generated a vicious circle. In the panel's judgment, national statistics that depend solely on sample surveys are unsustainable. There is little hope of maintaining information flow to the American public and decisionmakers without a fundamental change in the way statistics are produced.

The Digital Data Revolution Presents Opportunities and Challenges

While surveys and censuses are experiencing increasing risk of error and spiraling costs, other data are being produced at unprecedented rates by a variety of data holders. Some of these data arise from the operations of federal, state, and local government agencies—the "administrative records" that identify individuals or businesses, and the information they report to these programs or agencies (e.g., taxing authorities and benefit-payment providers). For example, linked administrative and survey data could provide insights about eligibility and access to the Supplemental Nutrition and Assistance Program (Bhaskar et al., 2021), or the impact of social security cutoffs on youth engagement with the criminal justice system could be

---

[2]See Czajka and Beyler (2016, p. 11) for discussion of reasons for declining response rates.

examined using a data infrastructure that integrates U.S. Census Bureau surveys and federal administrative data with state and local criminal justice administrative records (Deshpande and Mueller-Smith, 2022).[3] As another example, the effects of climate change could be measured by linking survey, census, and administrative data (Voorheis, 2021).

Administrative data from federal, state, and local governments can be an important source for statistical uses and evidence building (the National Academies, 2022b), and international statistical organizations are leveraging new data sources (Commission on Evidence-Based Policymaking, 2017; the National Academies, 2017b). In addition, local and city governments are already using data to make smarter, more informed decisions.[4] Yet, most of these federal, state, and local administrative-data assets remain untapped by the federal statistical system, and their use is often prohibited by statute for statistical uses or research.

Further, a much larger set of data is being produced in the private sector each minute, including vast amounts of transaction data—credit card transaction data, point-of-purchase information, customer loyalty programs, consumer purchasing histories, as well as troves of credit-monitoring data. The transaction data of e-commerce businesses includes product descriptions, prices, and quantity data, as well as information about the seller and purchaser, the transaction date, shipping location, and mode of transport. The housing market has also seen an explosion of data. Consumers can view satellite images of their homes and see their estimated values. They can shop, buy, sell, and arrange financing online. CoreLogic,[5] a data broker, has historic information on 5.5 billion property records, over one billion of which are updated every year. Online real estate brokers, like Redfin, use their data resources to produce housing-related statistics (Lambert, 2022). Health-related industries are also generating voluminous data. Electronic health records (EHRs) have grown exponentially and are shared among providers, clinicians, pharmacies, and patients. Acquiring and using EHRs in statistical surveys has been difficult (DeFrances and Lau, n.d.), but EHRs are available for other purposes. For example, the National Institutes of Health's All of Us[6] research program invited more than 1 million Americans to share their EHRs for research. The program recently released the first genomic dataset for 100,000 highly diverse whole-genome sequences (National Institutes of Health, 2022). Finally, mobile geolocation services embedded in nearly every app are another source of comprehensive

---

[3]The Criminal Justice Administrative Records System data infrastructure is described in Finlay et al., 2022.

[4]For examples, see: https://datasmart.ash.harvard.edu

[5]For more information, see: https://www.corelogic.com/why-corelogic/

[6]For more information, see: https://allofus.nih.gov/about/program-overview

individual data. These services can underpin individual mobility and provide data that can reveal intricate socio-behavioral phenomena (Valentino-DeVries et al., 2018). For example, retail scanner data have been used to determine household obesity status (Page et al., 2021).

The above examples illustrate the broad data revolution that is occurring and highlight current opportunities to enrich the data resources available for producing national statistics. Some new data sources contain data that households and businesses are asked to report in agency sample surveys, but they can also include more expansive and more timely data that could enrich existing statistical programs. Generally, these private sector data have been available to federal statistical agencies only through negotiated purchases or other bespoke contract mechanisms. Unlike federal and state administrative data, the use of private sector data is generally not limited by statute. These data have desirable properties that complement the attributes of surveys and censuses—almost all generate data in a more timely fashion than surveys. Further, some private sector data provide records of behavior, in contrast to survey responses in which accuracy may be impacted by a lack of records or respondent recall (Grotpeter, 2007; Biemer et al., 2013; Snijkers et al., 2013). Private sector data may also include information about segments of the population that are poorly represented in sample surveys.

However, these nonofficial data have weaknesses not shared by censuses and surveys produced by government agencies. Official censuses and surveys are designed to achieve the measurement needs of the agencies, covering well-defined populations. Administrative data are often designed for a specific purpose, such as tax administration, and may only cover a subset of the population (Liao et al., 2020). Furthermore, statutes generally protect privacy by limiting data access and uses to specified purposes. In contrast, data from the private sector are often generated for operational reasons (e.g., e-commerce transactions). These organizations aim to serve their customers; they do not attempt to collect similar data from an entire household population, from all producers, or for all products. For example, cash sales are often excluded from digitally available retail transaction data. Data from private sector firms typically only include data from their customers. Further, data from private sector companies and data holders can change over time in response to business needs, in ways inconsistent with a statistical program's needs for temporal consistency and comparability. Private sector data may disappear completely if business processes change, if a firm is sold or goes out of business, or if a firm simply decides to stop selling or sharing its data. Generally, commercial data are also limited in the number of attributes measured—they are often less descriptive than the multivariate richness provided by surveys and censuses. Additionally, private sector data may have quality issues or lack quality measures or adequate documentation.

Consequently, these two forms of data—responses (to surveys and censuses) and transactional records (from daily processes)—offer distinct strengths and weaknesses. Statistical surveys offer strong coverage of an entire population and measure many attributes on the sample units, but they are expensive, slow to produce information, and suffer from nonparticipation. Administrative data produced as part of federal or state programs are designed for a specific, nonstatistical purpose and, even if they achieve full participation, they might not represent the population. Local government and private sector organizations may offer more timely information, but only about those engaged in specific transactions or covered activities; these data may contain few attributes describing their customers. Similarly, data collected by nonprofit organizations and academic institutions or through crowdsourcing and citizen science have their particular strengths and weaknesses.

How can a data infrastructure take advantage of the strengths of these data assets and compensate for their weaknesses? Blended data combine information from at least two separate data assets. Careful blending of data from multiple, complementary sources, such as statistical surveys and censuses, administrative agencies, and the private sector, offers a way to generate more detailed, timely, and useful statistical information than is currently available (e.g., Tam et al., 2020).

Current Efforts to Use Digital Data to Repair Weaknesses in National Statistics Demonstrate the Possibilities and Limitations of Alternative Data Sources

The past several years have seen multiple attempts by researchers at statistical agencies to blend diverse data sources with existing survey and census data. Many of these collaborations are one-time agreements between holders of new digital resources and individual researchers.

Ron Jarmin (2019), U.S. Census Bureau, noted the important role that researchers have played in embracing alternative data sources:

> Unsurprisingly, researchers have been faster than the statistical agencies to adapt alternative, and especially government administrative data to various economic measurement tasks. There already have been a large increase in the utilization of administrative data for research (Chetty, 2012) and policy evaluation (Jarmin and O'Hara, 2016). Examples include analyses of trends in income inequality and the changing nature of business dynamics. Often these studies use administrative data to study patterns that simply are not available from existing survey-based data—moreover, would be prohibitively expensive to generate in a survey context. In the examples just mentioned, longitudinally linked microdata with universe coverage permit much more precise descriptions of the underlying dynamics than would be possible with survey data.

Importantly, these research efforts can and do lead to innovations in official statistical products. For example, early work on matched employer-employee data (Abowd, Haltiwanger, Lane, 2004) led to the development of the Quarterly Workforce Indicators which integrate many sources of information including administrative data from state unemployment insurance records and survey-based data from the American Community Survey[7] (Jarmin, 2019, p. 168).

Federal statistical agencies have recognized the importance of blending survey data with federal and state administrative data assets. BLS's Quarterly Census of Employment and Wages,[8] for example, blends survey data from the Multiple Worksite Report and the Annual Refilling Survey with administrative data provided by state unemployment insurance agencies. In a further extension, the U.S. Census Bureau's On the Map for Emergency Management,[9] an innovative byproduct of the matched employer-employee data mentioned above, integrates administrative, survey, and disaster-related real-time data from the National Weather Service's National Hurricane Center, the U.S. Department of the Interior, the U.S. Department of Agriculture, and the Federal Emergency Management Agency.

The panel's December 2021 workshops on The Scope, Components, and Key Characteristics of a 21st Century Data Infrastructure (see Appendix B for agendas) provided multiple examples of private sector data use by federal statistical agencies and units. All 13 designated statistical agencies, except for the Social Security Administration's Office of Research, Evaluation, and Statistics, are currently using private sector data assets (Reamer, 2021). The Bureau of Economic Analysis (BEA) uses some 142 private sector assets, and the Energy Information Administration (EIA) uses approximately 80 private sector data assets, while the U.S. Census Bureau uses approximately 20 private sector data sources. Extensive use of private sector data by BEA and EIA has long-standing historical roots—since the 1930s for BEA and the 1970s for EIA (Reamer, 2021). Statistical agencies reported that they use private sector data for multiple purposes, including "to supplement or combine with existing agency-held data" (82%), "to better understand other indicators of the economic environment" (71%), "for verification, quality control or quality assurance for existing data estimates" (53%), or to "continue current reporting capacity of agency practices" (53%; Reamer, 2021).

The growing practice of blending private sector data assets with administrative and survey data presents challenges for statistical agencies. These include costs, legal and procurement hurdles, problematic documentation,

---

[7]Note that references within this quote are from the cited source and are not included in the reference list for this report.
[8]See: https://www.bls.gov/cew/
[9]See: https://onthemap.ces.census.gov/em/

and data quality problems. In the workshop sessions, presenters highlighted the following challenges:

- Data acquisition, access, and use across the federal statistical system are fragmented, inefficient, sometimes redundant, and largely uncoordinated. Even within agencies, procurement processes can be time-consuming and complex.
- Using private sector data is currently difficult, challenging, and often expensive; inadequate or poorly documented metadata and technical obstacles make linking and blending data challenging.
- Laws and regulations remain major obstacles to accessing and using federal statistical agency-restricted data assets, federal program and administrative datasets, and state and local government datasets.
- Some data holders share their data, but vast spheres of activities have not yet been explored; shared data assets may not be representative.
- Data holders generally demand payment for data shared; costs vary significantly and sometimes increase substantially over time.
- Data-use agreements are often single-use and have no inherent replicability or sustainability.
- Data storage is siloed, expensive, and inefficient.
- The use of blended data requires new methods, statistical designs, privacy-preserving and confidentiality-protecting methods and tools, new skills and expertise, and possibly new organizational models.
- Privacy preservation and security protocols are inconsistent and vary across sectors, data holders, and agencies (the National Academies, 2017b, Ch. 5; O'Connor, 2018).

To meet these challenges in blending private sector data with surveys and other data sources, statistical agencies are actively sharing best practices and lessons learned. Such recent efforts to blend survey data with other data sources are consistent with the recommendations of several recent reports, detailed in the next section.

REPORTS RECOMMEND THE USE OF BLENDED DATA

Many recent studies evidence the need for blended data to improve statistical information. The first report of the National Academies' Panel on Improving Federal Statistics for Policy and Social Science Research Using Multiple Data Sources and State-of-the-Art Estimation Methods recommended combining data assets of federal, state, and local governments with private sector sources (the National Academies, 2017a, p. 44).

The report also recommended the creation of a new entity charged with facilitating access to and use of multiple data sources by statistical agencies and researchers (the National Academies, 2017a, p. 104). The panel's second report, issued in the fall of 2017, assessed alternative approaches for creating an environment that would blend diverse data sources (the National Academies, 2017b). The report described statistical methods and models needed to combine data; examined statistical and computer-science approaches that foster privacy protections; evaluated frameworks for assessing the quality and utility of alternative data sources; and considered various options for implementing a new organization to facilitate data sharing.

A report from the Markle Foundation (2021) also supported the use of blended data to better meet the needs of policymakers, researchers, and the public. This report found that "reducing barriers and increasing capacity could significantly advance privacy-protected data sharing, help address disparity and inequality, and improve knowledge on how to increase economic mobility" (Markle Foundation, 2021, p. 4). During 2020, the Markle team conducted five expert working-group sessions and multiple one-on-one calls with experts to identify opportunities fostered by an improved data ecosystem:[10]

- Increasing equity in federal data, to better understand and address racial disparity and other inequities;
- Improving the accessibility and use of state data, to obtain insights into programs and benefits provided at the state level and to allow state and local policymakers to better understand and meet needs across geographies and populations;
- Increasing engagement with the public and community stakeholders on data collection, use, and reuse; and
- Leveraging new data (including private sector data), and creating new economic measures.

Active research and development projects are also helping to propel the use of blended data to improve government statistics and address issues of national importance. One example is the recently announced modernization of the U.S. Census Bureau's residential construction statistics program, which was possible only by blending multiple data sources (Darr, 2022). Rather than collecting residential housing permits, which would include data from 9,000 permit-issuing organizations, the U.S. Census Bureau will

---

[10]The Markle team used a slightly different terminology in its report than is used here. It focused on the government or federal "data ecosystem," not a vision of a new national data infrastructure.

receive data from third-party sources and introduce a small cutoff sample to supplement the third-party data. Satellite imagery (using geolocation/georeferenced data dimensions), rather than data collected by telephone interviewers, will be used to identify the start of construction. This approach was adopted after collaborating with Statistics Canada. When fully implemented, the U.S. Census Bureau will publish more granular statistics, including construction permit statistics for every jurisdiction in the U.S., rather than just for states.

A second example illustrates that data sharing may advance understanding of current supply-chain bottlenecks. While existing statistical surveys and programs (including import and export statistics) collect data from important supply-chain participants, these statistics do not illuminate supply-chain logistics. A recent White House/industry partnership, the Freight Logistics Optimization Works project, is a data-sharing initiative that will pilot data exchanges between parts of the goods-movement supply chain, to produce a proof-of-concept by the end of summer 2022 (The White House, 2022a). The supply-chain pilot may provide insights about bottlenecks that cannot be gleaned from statistical surveys or programs, but additional benefits may be possible by linking pilot results with existing survey-based data and administrative data sources. Such linking could provide additional insights into the characteristics of key supply-chain participants.

Despite evidence that the blending of diverse data assets for statistical purposes is already a growing component of the federal statistical system and other parts of government,[11] there is no cohesive, coordinated plan to build a new data infrastructure to provide statistical agencies or the broader community access to the diverse, relevant data sources needed to further this practice. The current state of the national data infrastructure prevents the United States from fully realizing the promise of blended data. A new national data infrastructure is needed that supports and facilitates the use of blended data to produce more timely, granular, and useful information.

RECENT CONGRESSIONAL AND DATA-RELATED INITIATIVES: NECESSARY BUT NOT SUFFICIENT

The important work of the Commission on Evidence-Based Policymaking (CEP) resulted in statutory change. CEP was established in 2016 to develop a strategy for increasing the availability and use of government data

---

[11] The Federal Geographic Data Committee has been dealing with blending geospatial data for some time as Ivan DeLoach, workshop participant and former director of the Federal Geographic Data Committee, noted at The Scope, Components, and Key Characteristics of a 21st Century Data Infrastructure Workshop on December 9th, 2021.

to build evidence about government programs while protecting privacy and confidentiality. The Commission's report, *The Promise of Evidence-Based Policymaking,* includes numerous recommendations for improving data access in a secure, privacy- and confidentiality-protected manner; modernizing privacy protections for evidence-building; implementing a National Secure Data Service (a service provider, not a data warehouse) within the U.S. Department of Commerce; and strengthening federal evidence-building capacity (Commission on Evidence-Based Policymaking, 2017). CEP used the phrase "evidence" to mean the use of statistical information for evaluating alternative policy decisions faced by the government's executive and legislative branches. More broadly, however, CEP recommendations also focus on improving access and use of federal and state government-collected and federally controlled data for statistical purposes, including statistical production, research, and evidence-building activities. As a result of CEP's report, the president signed the Foundations for Evidence-Based Policymaking Act of 2018 (hereafter, the Evidence Act) on January 14th, 2019 (U.S. Congress, 2019). The Evidence Act implemented about half of CEP's recommendations and provides statistical agencies with a broader statutory basis for accessing and using data assets of federal nonstatistical agencies: "The head of an agency shall, to the extent practicable, make any data asset maintained by the agency available, upon request, to any statistical agency or unit for purposes of developing evidence" (U.S. Congress, 2019, Section 3581(a)).

The Evidence Act also expanded secure access to datasets covered by the Confidential Information Protection and Statistical Efficiency Act for approved statistical purposes, including evidence and evaluation uses, consistent with existing laws and regulations (U.S. Congress, 2002a, Section 3582). The Evidence Act encourages sharing, for statistical purposes, and among designated federal agencies and entities, of data assets "created by, collected by, under the control or direction of, or maintained by the (federal) agency" (U.S. Congress, 2019, Section 3511(a)(1)), consistent with existing laws and regulations.

Title II of the Evidence Act establishes open data as the default for public data assets, unless restrictions or limitations exist, such as protecting confidentiality or national security. The Evidence Act requires agencies (statistical and nonstatistical) to develop and maintain a comprehensive inventory of all federally held and controlled data assets (including metadata) and access privileges. The Evidence Act also requires the U.S. Office of Management and Budget (OMB) to issue regulations on data classification by federal agencies, according to data sensitivity, and to provide access accordingly. Finally, the Evidence Act requires federal agencies to develop evidence-based policy and evaluation plans and to designate evaluation officers, statistical officials, and chief data officers to support and implement these new requirements.

The director of OMB was directed to establish a standard access process "through which agencies, the Congressional Budget Office, State, local, and Tribal governments, researchers, and other individuals, as appropriate, may apply to access the data assets accessed or acquired under this subchapter by a statistical agency or unit for purposes of developing evidence" (U.S. Congress, 2019, Section 3583).

According to the Evidence Act, providing access to data assets is "for purposes of developing evidence." The Evidence Act defines "evidence" as "information produced as a result of statistical activities conducted for a statistical purpose" (U.S. Congress, 2019). OMB later provided federal agencies with additional guidance regarding Evidence Act implementation and broadly defined "evidence" to include:

- Foundational fact-finding—foundational research and analysis, such as aggregate indicators, exploratory studies, descriptive statistics, and basic research;
- Performance measurement—ongoing, systematic tracking of information relevant to policies, strategies, programs, projects, goals/objectives, and/or activities;
- Policy analysis—analysis of data, such as general-purpose surveys or program-specific data, to generate and inform policy (e.g., estimating regulatory impacts and other effects); and
- Program evaluation—a systematic analysis of a program, policy, organization, or components of these, to evaluate effectiveness and efficiency (OMB, 2019). In short, any of these uses would meet the Evidence Act's definition of a legitimate "statistical purpose."

The Evidence Act also established the Advisory Committee on Data for Evidence Building (ACDEB), which currently has 26 members from federal agencies, state and local governments, academia, nonprofits, and the private sector. ACDEB is directed to "...evaluate and provide recommendations to the Director [of OMB] on how to facilitate data sharing, enable data linkage, and develop privacy enhancing techniques" (U.S. Congress, 2019). The first meeting of ACDEB was held in October 2020, and the Committee met monthly through November 2021 and bi-monthly thereafter. ACDEB is scheduled to terminate in October 2022.

On June 28th, 2021, the U.S. House of Representatives passed the bipartisan National Science Foundation for the Future Act (U.S. Congress, 2021)[12] that included the National Secure Data Service (NSDS) Act. The NSDS Act directs the National Science Foundation (NSF) director, in consultation with the chief statistician, to establish a demonstration project

---

[12]The NSDS Act was not acted on by the U.S. Senate and, thus, did not become law.

within a year of enactment, to "develop, refine, and test models to inform the full implementation of the CEP recommendations for government-wide data linkage and access infrastructure for statistical activities conducted for statistical purposes."[13] At a January 21st, 2022, ACDEB meeting, NSF announced that America's DataHub Consortium (ADC) would be the demonstration project and would be located in the National Center for Science and Engineering Statistics within NSF (Arora, 2022). At a meeting on May 20th, 2022, it was reiterated that ADC would be the pilot for the NSDS. On August 9th, 2022, the president signed the CHIPS and Science Act of 2022, which authorized and funded an unnamed NSDS demonstration project with language nearly identical to that used in the original NSDS Act. Section 10375 of the CHIPS and Science Act "establishes a National Secure Data Service demonstration project to test models and inform the full implementation of a government-wide data linkage and access infrastructure" (U.S. Congress, 2022a).

ACDEB issued a Year 1 Report on October 29th, 2021, including recommendations and a roadmap for Year 2 activities (Advisory Committee on Data for Evidence Building, 2021). At the ACDEB meeting on January 21st, 2022, OMB and the Interagency Council on Statistical Policy (ICSP) verbally responded to the Year 1 Report, announcing that they would engage with ACDEB iteratively, focusing on the Standard Access Process, ADC, and several other ICSP initiatives. It is unclear how this new iterative approach will influence the ACDEB Year 2 Roadmap included in the October 2021 Year 1 report. Consistent with the Evidence Act and CEP, ACDEB did not address possible improvements through the use of private sector data for national statistics.

ACDEB discussed the Biden Administration's priorities, including presidential memoranda and executive orders that impact the Panel's work (The White House, 2021a,b). The Executive Order on Advancing Racial Equity established the Equitable Data Working Group, an interagency group co-chaired by the U.S. chief statistician and the U.S. chief technology officer, to identify "inadequacies in existing Federal data collection programs, policies, and infrastructure across agencies, and strategies for addressing any inadequacies identified" (The White House, 2021b). The Equitable Data Working Group[14] released its recommendations in a report issued on April 22nd, 2022 (The White House, 2022b). The second report in this

---

[13]Excerpted from full bill text: https://www.congress.gov/bill/117th-congress/house-bill/3133/text

[14]The Equitable Data Working Group's activities and recommendations were reviewed by the panel, but did not contribute to the report.

series, *The Implications of Using Multiple Data Sources for Major Survey Programs,* will discuss data equity issues.[15]

SUMMARY

While the federal statistical system is still heavily dependent on surveys and censuses, the survey-centric paradigm faces major challenges associated with declining response rates, rising costs, and the inability of budgets to keep pace with increasing data demands. Administrative data sources have been leveraged by some statistical programs, especially business statistics programs such as the Economic Census and BLS's Quarterly Census of Employment and Wages program.

The examples of statistical agencies using blended data—both those described in this chapter and those discussed during the National Academies' December 2021 workshops on The Scope, Components, and Key Characteristics of a 21st Century Data Infrastructure—have shown promising results. However, broader use is often limited by statute, complicated negotiations and contract mechanisms, lack of methods or expertise, or unwillingness to share data. It is indisputable that the opportunities are prodigious. While the Evidence Act provided statistical agencies with a broader statutory basis for accessing and using data assets of federal nonstatistical agencies (U.S. Congress, 2019, Section 3581), more than two years after its enactment, a major advance has not been achieved.

The United States needs a new 21st century national data infrastructure that blends data from multiple sources to improve the quality, timeliness, granularity, and usefulness of national statistics, facilitates more rigorous social and economic research, and supports evidence-based policymaking and program evaluations. (Conclusion 2-1)

State, local, territory, and tribal governments also have data assets that could benefit the federal statistical system. CEP recognizes the importance of state administrative data, but its state-related recommendations were not enacted. Consequently, statistical agency access to many state and local data assets is limited by statute; in some cases, access is limited or constrained by the lack of resources and expertise of state and local governments. ACDEB has discussed at length the importance of state and local government data assets for the federal data ecosystem. In the panel's opinion, state and local

---

[15]For a video recording of the May 16th and May 18th workshop, see: https://www.nationalacademies.org/event/05-16-2022/the-implications-of-using-multiple-data-sources-for-major-survey-programs-workshop

government data assets are an essential component of a new national data infrastructure.

A key portion of the National Academies' December 2021 workshops on The Scope, Components, and Key Characteristics of a 21st Century Data Infrastructure focused on statistical agencies' uses of private sector data for official statistics and research. CEP, the Evidence Act, and ACDEB deliberations and recommendations do not identify private sector data as a key component of a new national data infrastructure. Workshop participants noted that private sector data utilization for national purposes might greatly improve the quality, timeliness, and granularity of national statistics, as well as improve knowledge of groups that are not well represented in existing surveys. Private sector data can also support important scientific discoveries by facilitating rigorous research, and recent expert groups have recommended the inclusion of private sector data. In the panel's judgment, private sector data assets are an essential component of a new data infrastructure. Untapping private data sources poses challenges but also provides unique opportunities to improve national statistics by leveraging existing information and blending it with other data sources.

This chapter has illustrated that blending multiple data sources to produce new statistics is a growing practice of the federal statistical system and needs support to expand further. The data assets available for blending in a new data infrastructure include those held by the federal statistical, program, and administrative agencies; state, tribal, territory, and local governments; private sector companies; nonprofit and academic institutions; and crowdsourced and citizen-science data. At this time, however, the United States has no cohesive, coordinated plan to ensure that novel, blended data become an essential and growing source of public information and research. The current state of the national data infrastructure prevents a realization of the promise of blended data. Data acquisition, access, and use are siloed, inefficient, and largely uncoordinated. Laws and regulations remain major obstacles to accessing and using federal statistical, program, and administrative data as well as state, local, and tribal government data. Private sector data use is bespoke and often costly, with no inherent sustainability. Most data holders have no incentives to contribute or share their data for the common good. Privacy-protecting behaviors of data holders are highly variable and largely unregulated, and there is little transparency and accountability for private sector data use.

In the panel's judgment, the current national data infrastructure is ill-equipped to meet the data needs of the 21st century. The reliance on the federal statistical system on statistical surveys as a primary data source is unsustainable. To meet the demands for credible, trustworthy, and timely statistical information, the United States needs a new data infrastructure that facilitates the increased blending of data from multiple sources.

3

A Vision for a
New National Data Infrastructure

Statistical agencies are largely siloed, they heavily rely on surveys as the primary source of data, and they independently identify and negotiate access to new data assets. Blending survey data with other data sources is the exception, not the rule, and data products that incorporate blended data are rare. Laws and regulations remain major obstacles to accessing and using federal statistical, program, and administrative data, as well as state, tribal, territory, and local government data. Most data holders have no incentives to contribute or share their data for the common good.

Statistical agencies depend primarily on survey data, with limited use of administrative and state-provided or local government data, and efforts to use private sector data are largely uncoordinated. Information flows are unidirectional (from data holders to statistical agencies), with only limited data sharing among statistical agencies. Currently, there is little cross-agency access to data and minimal, if any, access to federal and state administrative data for evidence building. While there are 31 federal statistical research data centers (FSRDCs)—highly secure sites for approved in-person and virtual research using federal statistical agency data—located across the United States, statistical agency participation is not universal. These FSRDCs, importantly, facilitate collaborative agreements between more than a hundred universities, the entire Federal Reserve System, and four principal statistical agencies. However, no statistical organization has overall responsibility for coordinating data access and use among data holders, statistical agencies, and data users. In the panel's view, the mismatch between the vision of a 21st century national data infrastructure and its current state is stark, and the gap will continue to grow unless attention is focused on identifying and implementing important attributes for a new data infrastructure.

This chapter begins by describing a vision for a new data infrastructure, the expected outcomes, and a description of seven key data-infrastructure attributes. As highways and bridges have little value without facilitating commerce and social interaction, a data infrastructure gains its value by its use, permitting organizations, entities, and functions that use it and its products to build better information.

VISION FOR A 21ST CENTURY NATIONAL DATA INFRASTRUCTURE

The panel's vision for a new data infrastructure assumes that statistical agencies and other approved users (federal, state, tribal, territory, and local government employees and researchers) will access and use data assets relevant to the nation's information and research needs for the common good. These include data assets of federal statistical, program, and administrative agencies; state, tribal, territory, and local governments; private sector companies; nonprofit, tax-exempt, and academic institutions; and crowdsourced and citizen-science data. Operations using a new infrastructure would blend multiple data sources to improve the quality, timeliness, granularity, and usefulness of national statistics; facilitate more rigorous social and economic research; and support evidence-based policymaking and program evaluation. Access and use for solely statistical purposes will require approval, will comply with existing laws and regulations, and will be governed by established policies, rules, and procedures.

In the panel's vision, explicit values will guide the operations of a new data infrastructure and decisions relating to its use. Primary among these values is respecting and protecting data subjects and data holders. Other values are articulated in *Principles and Practices for a Federal Statistical Agency* (the National Academies of Sciences, Engineering, and Medicine, 2021) and include producing information relevant to societal issues, credibility among users, public trust, independence from political influence, and continual innovation. To achieve these values, strengthened data safeguards will secure data, preserve privacy, and protect confidentiality of data subjects. These safeguards will minimize the harm to any individual or data subject, but will maximize the infrastructure's benefits to society.

Safeguard mechanisms and measures will be communicated widely— in the panel's vision, transparency is central to the success of a new data infrastructure. The public, data holders, and data subjects will be able to see how their data are used, by whom, for what purposes, and to what societal benefit. This will generate confidence that data are used responsibly, ethically, and only for approved statistical purposes.

Data infrastructure operations and decisions must, in the panel's judgment, be consistent with professional principles and practices and with ethical standards, and must be autonomous and free of political interference.[1] The data infrastructure must be inclusive—the public, data holders, data subjects, and other important constituencies must be engaged in standards development, data governance, and other pertinent decisions, strengthening trust in the data infrastructure. The new data infrastructure must not only provide tangible benefits for the common good, but also ensure societal benefits are proportionate to the possible costs and risks of acquiring and using data assets.

In the panel's vision, a new data infrastructure must also support two-way information flows: from data holders to statistical agencies and from statistical agencies to data holders. Statistical agencies must return useful information and services to data holders to inform the data holders' decisions, operations, and activities. In turn, the public, data holders, and key stakeholders must support legislation and other changes that facilitate and support expanded data access and use.

Outcomes of a New Data Infrastructure

According to the panel's vision, a new data infrastructure would strengthen, improve, and transform the ways the United States uses and benefits from richer informational resources, providing new capabilities and much-needed capacity building (see Box 3-1).

Key Attributes of a New Data Infrastructure

The stark differences between the state of the current data infrastructure and the panel's vision for a new data infrastructure prevent the United States from effectively utilizing vast amounts of available data that could provide more timely, granular, and useful information to support more rigorous research. These data could also support evidence-based evaluations and analysis of federal, tribal, state, and local governments' policies and programs. This mismatch between the current reality and the panel's vision will continue to grow, in the panel's opinion, unless attention is focused on establishing a new data infrastructure with a set of key attributes.

Box 3-2 presents seven key attributes of a 21st century national data infrastructure, as envisioned by the panel. The remainder of the chapter

---

[1]In this chapter and throughout the report, when the panel discusses "professional principles and practices" in compiling national statistics—either within the existing federal statistical system or a new data infrastructure—it considers the National Academies (2021) as an authoritative source of such information.

BOX 3-1
Outcomes of a New Data Infrastructure

- The nation's information resources are strengthened by blending data from multiple data sources and employing new methods, designs, capabilities, technology, and tools.
- Critical information for decisionmakers is made more timely, granular, and useful by expanding access to data from a broader set of data holders.
- Researchers illuminate issues of national importance by accessing existing data assets.
- Enhanced evidence-based policy analysis informs federal, state, tribal, territory, and local governments.
- Data holders are incentivized to share data for statistical purposes, by the provision of tangible benefits that inform and improve their operations and activities.
- A reformed legal and regulatory framework undergirds protections for both participants and authorities, permitting increased use of existing data resources for common-good statistical information.
- The national data infrastructure operates in a high-trust environment, characterized by transparency, that balances expanded data use with strengthened privacy preservation and confidentiality protection, data security, legal compliance, and responsible and ethical data use.

SOURCE: Panel generated.

BOX 3-2
Seven Attributes of a 21st Century
National Data Infrastructure Vision

1. **Safeguards and advanced privacy-enhancing practices** to minimize possible individual harm.
2. **Statistical uses only**, for common-good information, with statistical aggregates freely shared with all.
3. **Mobilization of relevant digital data assets**, blended in statistical aggregates to providing benefits to data holders, with societal benefits proportionate to possible costs and risks.
4. **Reformed legal authorities** protecting all parties' interests.
5. **Governance framework and standards** effectively supporting operations.
6. **Transparency to the public** regarding analytical operations using the infrastructure.
7. **State-of-the-art practices** for access, statistical, coordination, and computational activities; continuously improved to efficiently create increasingly secure and useful information.

SOURCE: Panel generated.

describes changes necessary to produce the required attributes supporting a new data infrastructure.

ATTRIBUTES OF A NEW DATA INFRASTRUCTURE

Attribute 1: Safeguards and Advanced Privacy-Enhancing Practices to Minimize Possible Individual Harm

Per the panel's vision, a new data infrastructure needs strong, uniform privacy protections for data and needs to account for the presence, interests, and rights of data subjects. The current infrastructure does neither, in the panel's judgment. For example, the protection of the autonomy of individuals and data subjects to oversee which data are accessed and how they are used is vastly different between the private and government sectors, and there is a wide diversity in privacy protections across states. Federal program agencies, which use their data resources mainly for administrative purposes, have scattered, diverse, and occasionally arcane regulations. It is not surprising, therefore, that United States residents have little understanding of the data protections that exist under a given set of circumstances or regarding a specific organization.

In the panel's opinion, a new data infrastructure should be oriented around the data subjects and the ways digital data connected to those subjects are affecting their lives (Beauchamp and Childress, 2001). First, the infrastructure must avoid causing personal harm. Individual data should only be combined to produce aggregate descriptions of groups or to help model estimates. Access to individual records must not be allowed.

Second, the panel argues that a new data infrastructure must address underlying issues of autonomy—the ability of data subjects to make their own decisions. As a new data infrastructure is developed, how will individuals and the community at large be involved with the creation of consent procedures relevant to blending multiple data sources to produce aggregate statistics? The infrastructure must recognize that data subjects may be unaware of informed consent requirements, have differing privacy stances, and may grapple with the ethical dimensions of data usage. Just because data *can* be accessed does not mean that they should be used.

Third, the panel believes that the public should have a beneficent view of a new data infrastructure. Data subjects need to understand how data will be used to produce good outcomes for them. The goal of a new data infrastructure must be to provide information on critical societal and economic topics; thus, the ability to produce individual benefits derived from improved information about the country's health, education, income, and safety will be the cornerstone of the infrastructure's appeal. To engender trust in a new data infrastructure, it is imperative that the government actively communicate with the public about the importance of the infrastructure and its activities.

Fourth, in the panel's vision, a new data infrastructure must reinforce human dignity. That is, the uses of the new infrastructure should be respectful of the data subjects. The infrastructure's key values must place the data subject at the center, even as the infrastructure focuses on the societal benefits that can be derived from using the subject's data to produce aggregate statistical information for the good of society.

In short, accounting for data subjects and their rights, minimizing possible harm, and broadly engaging communities are ethical necessities that will contribute to the legitimacy and trust-building required for a successful new data infrastructure. Privacy and security are key features of a trusted system; data are safeguarded and secured, while privacy is preserved and confidentiality protected. Thus, a new data infrastructure will implement a strong set of safeguards to assure data will not be used to harm any individual or data subject. A combination of modern cybersecurity, encryption, and secure access protocols can provide greatly enhanced data security, while new privacy-enhancing technologies are essential for protecting the confidentiality of subjects' data. If strong protections are in place, the panel notes that the societal benefits of statistical information critical to society's welfare will not come at the price of increased threats to privacy and confidentiality. Minimal collection of new data is envisioned for a new data infrastructure; instead, such an infrastructure would involve expanded and responsible use of existing data to produce high-quality information about crucial societal features.

Most existing legal protections of personal and organizational data lie at the federal government level. The Confidential Information Protection and Statistical Efficiency Act (CIPSEA) was first enacted as Title V of the E-Government Act of 2002 (U.S. Congress, 2002a). For all data furnished by individuals or organizations to an agency under a pledge of confidentiality, Subtitle A provides that the data will be used only for statistical purposes and will not be disclosed in identifiable form to anyone not authorized by the title. CIPSEA makes the knowing, willful disclosure of confidential statistical data a class E felony, with fines of up to $250,000 and imprisonment for up to five years. Data held by the U.S. Census Bureau are protected by Title 13, which specifies similar protections (U.S. Census Bureau, n.d.). Appendix 3A, taken from *Principles and Practices for a Federal Statistical Agency* (the National Academies, 2021), reviews the various laws affecting the operations of the federal agencies.

Existing laws for federal statistical agencies imply that protecting data can offer a data subject complete certainty of nondisclosure. This contradicts the modern understanding that the risk of disclosure can never be driven to zero. Modern privacy-protecting procedures offer ways to measure and limit the risk of disclosing or reconstructing an individual's data. Further, cybersecurity methods continue to evolve to offer greater protections. Finally, sustainable methods have evolved for using data for research and solely statistical purposes, without violating confidentiality pledges given by federal statistical agencies (for example the FSRDC network).[2] A new data infrastructure can take advantages of these discoveries in mounting its privacy-protecting framework.

The panel also observed large variations in current data protection. Some data resources relevant to social and economic statistics are well protected, while others are not. As the construction of a new data infrastructure proceeds, stronger, more uniform data protections will necessarily be built, which will improve the privacy of existing data resources. Thus, a new data infrastructure could be a net gain to the privacy protections of the United States population and enterprises. The privacy and ethical implications of blended data are explored in Chapter 4, as this will be a critical feature of a new data infrastructure.

> It is ethically necessary and technically possible to preserve privacy and fulfill confidentiality pledges regarding data while simultaneously expanding the statistical uses of diverse data sources. (Conclusion 3-1)

Attribute 2: Statistical Uses Only, for Common-Good Information, with Statistical Aggregates Freely Shared with All

In the panel's opinion, the sustainability of a new national data infrastructure rests on its use for statistical purposes *only*. In essence, a new data infrastructure has the sole aim of serving the common good of society; its operations and decisions are consistent with professional principles and practices, conform to ethical standards, and are autonomous and free of political interference. In the panel's vision of a new infrastructure, only statistical aggregates, estimates, or synthetic microdata would be released, describing the state of health, income, education, employment, safety, transportation, business, food security, environment, and housing. The data assets would be available for advanced research to guide improvements in each of these sectors. The statistical information produced would be freely shared with all parts of society and would help shape the national discourse, informing the practical actions of decisionmakers in all sectors and guiding institutional policies at all levels.

No use of the data should allow identification of an individual, household, business, or specific data subject, in the panel's opinion. No individual records used for statistical purposes should be accessible to any

---

[2]For more information, see: https://www.census.gov/about/adrm/fsrdc.html

governmental or law enforcement agency. Confidential data should not be used as part of any intervention or for enforcement of any laws or regulations affecting a data subject. In the panel's view, creation of statistical information that is useful for society and decisionmakers must be the only goal of a new data infrastructure. The Foundations for Evidence-Based Policymaking Act (hereafter, Evidence Act) defines statistical purpose to include "description, estimation, or analysis of the characteristics of groups, without identifying the individuals or organizations that comprise such groups; and includes the development, implementation, or maintenance of methods, technical or administrative procedures, or information resources that support the [statistical] purpose" (U.S. Congress, 2019, Section 3561 (12)).

In contrast, the Evidence Act defines a nonstatistical purpose as using data in identifiable form for:

> ...administrative, regulatory, law enforcement, adjudicatory, or other purposes that affects the rights, privileges, and benefits of a particular identifiable respondent and includes the disclosure under section 552 of title 5 (popularly known as the Freedom of Information Act) of data that are acquired for exclusively statistical purposes under a pledge of confidentiality (U.S. Congress, 2019, Section 3561 (8)).

The panel stands by both definitions in arguing for statistical uses only. To clarify, statistical uses of collected or acquired income data, for example, would include calculating aggregate statistics, computing income distributions, or showing the number of households below the poverty line. Such uses would include constructing models to produce estimates or to construct synthetic populations. The statistical-only purposes of a new data infrastructure would not prevent a federal administrative agency from collecting the same income data and using it to determine program eligibility—to grant or deny benefits to individuals based on income. However, that agency could not obtain such records directly from a new data infrastructure.

Determinations of statistical purposes for federal statistical agencies have, generally, been relatively straightforward, but the Evidence Act has added a wrinkle relevant to a new national data infrastructure. The Evidence Act provides access to data assets "for purposes of developing evidence," where "evidence" is "information produced as a result of statistical activities conducted for a statistical purpose" (U.S. Congress, 2019, Section 3561(6)).

As mentioned in Chapter 2, the U.S. Office of Management and Budget (OMB) memorandum M-19-23 (U.S. Office of Management and Budget, 2019) provides federal agencies with additional guidance regarding Evidence Act implementation and defines "evidence" broadly. OMB guidance suggests the following legitimate statistical purposes: statistical production and dissemination (aggregate statistics), approved research, policy analysis, program evaluation, and performance measurement of key data infrastructure operations and activities. The panel notes that all of these are uses of statistical data appropriate for a new data infrastructure.

Federal statistical agencies have legally sanctioned missions limited to statistical uses of data. The panel sees the statistical agencies identified in Box 3-3 playing an important role in a new data infrastructure, but they should not be the only participants, in the panel's estimation. Data holders, data users, researchers, and entities involved in data infrastructure

---

BOX 3-3
Designated U.S. Federal Statistical Agencies and Units

- Bureau of Economic Analysis (U.S. Department of Commerce)
- Bureau of Justice Statistics (U.S. Department of Justice)
- Bureau of Labor Statistics (U.S. Department of Labor)
- Bureau of Transportation Statistics (U.S. Department of Transportation)
- Census Bureau (U.S. Department of Commerce)
- Economic Research Service (U.S. Department of Agriculture)
- Energy Information Administration (U.S. Department of Energy)
- National Agricultural Statistics Service (U.S. Department of Agriculture)
- National Center for Education Statistics (U.S. Department of Education)
- National Center for Health Statistics (U.S. Department of Health and Human Services)
- National Center for Science and Engineering Statistics (National Science Foundation)
- Office of Research, Evaluation, and Statistics (Social Security Administration) Statistics of Income Division (Internal Revenue Service)

Using criteria from the 2007 Confidential Information Protection and Statistical Efficiency Act of 2002 (CIPSEA), the U.S. Office of Management and Budget recognized four additional units as statistical units for purposes of CIPSEA:

- Office of Research, Evaluation, and Statistics (Social Security Administration unit included to provide CIPSEA coverage and protection)
- Center for Behavioral Health Statistics and Quality of the Substance Abuse and Mental Health Services Administration (U.S. Department of Health and Human Services)
- Microeconomics Surveys Section (Federal Reserve Board)
- National Animal Health Monitoring System Program Unit of the Animal and Plant Health Inspection Service (U.S. Department of Agriculture)

SOURCE: Adapted from the National Academies (2021, pp. 105–106).

coordination, collaboration, governance, and accountability will all have important roles in realizing the promise of a new data infrastructure. New actors will only be permitted data access if the data are to be used for approved statistical purposes. Moreover, data infrastructure operations and decisions will be consistent with professional principles and practices, as previously explained.

Attribute 3: Mobilization of Relevant National Digital Data Assets, Blended in Statistical Aggregates to Provide Benefits to Data Holders, with Societal Benefits Proportionate to Possible Costs and Risks

To achieve the panel's vision, a new national data infrastructure would provide access to a variety of currently collected digital assets when those data are relevant to the nation's information and research needs. Thus, in the panel's vision, a new data infrastructure will mobilize and leverage the strategic value of national data resources in a coordinated way (Box 3-4). A new data infrastructure will gather information from all relevant sectors to assist the development of society as a whole. These data-holder assets are fully described in Chapter 4, along with their strengths, weaknesses, and any statutory limitations on their access and use.

As the blending of data becomes a key component of a new data infrastructure, the infrastructure will include a wider variety of data holders, data subjects, data seekers, and data users than in the past, necessitating new relationships, partnerships, and collaborations. Thus, the need to demonstrate the benefits of expanded data sharing to diverse data holders and important stakeholders becomes a prerequisite for the success of a new data infrastructure. State, tribal, territory, and local governments, along

---

BOX 3-4
Data Holders Proposed to Share Data in a
21st Century National Data Infrastructure

- Principal federal statistical agencies
- Federal program and administrative agencies
- State, tribal, territory, and local governments
- Private sector enterprises
- Data brokers
- Nonprofit and academic institutions
- Crowdsourced or citizen science

SOURCE: Panel generated.

with private sector companies and other data holders, will be more likely to share their data assets for approved statistical purposes if they understand the tangible benefits that expanded sharing provides both to themselves and to society.

At the National Academies' December 2021 workshops on The Scope, Components, and Key Characteristics of a 21st Century Data Infrastructure, the panel was presented with potential benefits of a new data infrastructure, including the promise of more timely, better quality, and more granular statistics that could answer questions of national interest, support more rigorous research, and facilitate evidence-based policymaking. However, in the panel's opinion, benefits should go beyond improved statistics to include reciprocal information sharing, in which tailored insights extracted from data assets and analysis flow back to data holders, informing their activities and operations.

Direct Benefits to Data Holders of Sharing Data for National Statistical Purposes

The panel reviewed a set of benefits that could sustainably be offered to data holders in return for access to their data for national statistical needs. First, it is of great interest to many private sector firms and administrative units that data sharing be consistent with user agreements pledged to clients whose data they hold. Nathan Persily, workshop participant, noted that the proposed Platform Transparency and Accountability Act[3] provides qualified platforms with limited legal liability if they comply with the act's specified privacy and cybersecurity provisions. A similar liability provision could incentivize companies and other data holders to share their data by protecting them against possible legal threats related to data sharing.

Second, all organizations are facing the continuous threat of intruders into their data systems. Small- and medium-sized private sector firms might profit from a set of continuously updated cybersecurity services provided by a new data infrastructure that would improve protection of the firms' core business information, concomitant with the sharing of their data. Such a benefit might serve two purposes: the strengthening of privacy protections for data accessed by the infrastructure, and a tangible incentive to private sector firms that assuages concerns about breaches that might result from a data-sharing agreement.

Third, when businesses can compare their performance to other businesses in their sectors (e.g., using standard product definitions, industrial classification definitions, definitions of urban areas), clear value results.

---

[3]The proposed law has not been enacted as of June 2022. See Wright (2021) for more information.

If statistical information were available on all organizations in a sector, business officials could benchmark their activities and easily compare the performance of their enterprise to that of similar enterprises. The standard classification systems have informed organization decisionmaking, and, to the extent that common definitions, standards, and classification can evolve through a new data infrastructure, participating organizations could interoperate with one another and compare data discoveries. Such curation benefits are discussed later in this chapter.

Fourth, according to the panel, financial incentives must be considered. Federal government requests for information impose a burden on respondents. This burden is the foundation of the Paperwork Reduction Act requirements stating that federal agencies must publish the justification for, and the estimated burden related to, their information requests (U.S. Congress, 1995). Currently, the ongoing efforts of blending private sector data with other data resources generally involve payment of funds from the data-seeking organization to the data holder. For some data-holding organizations, the fees simply cover transaction costs. However, other data holders regard these fees as a revenue stream that is part of their business model. Tax incentives to reduce total costs incurred by data sharing are another financial incentive that could be considered for data holders in a new data infrastructure.

Fifth, private sector organizations are constantly searching for useful information about the future of their enterprises and changes in their customer bases. Participation in a new data infrastructure could influence the production of more timely statistical products than those currently available. Given the common-good purposes of a new data infrastructure as envisioned by the panel, new statistical products would be shared publicly and not merely provided to those who share their data, but the infrastructure should look for ways to formally acknowledge data sharing. However, a new data infrastructure could usher in a new era of information flow back to businesses, nonprofits, and government organizations. Timely, granular statistical information to assist with modern forecasting analyses could be of ubiquitous benefit to growing the economy and improving society. Such a new era would begin with the promise that a new data infrastructure would be designed to benefit data subjects, data holders, data users, and society as a whole.

Another way to incentivize data holders is to ensure that the societal benefits are proportionate to the possible costs and risks of sharing their data assets. Such costs and risks are of major concern for data holders. For example, Statistics Canada's proposal to use private sector financial information for statistical purposes, though perfectly legal, resulted in such a public outcry that the project was abandoned, and Statistics Canada added "sensitivity" to its "necessity and proportionality" framework (Bowlby,

2021). Ensuring that the benefits of data sharing are proportionate to the associated costs and risks will require a new data infrastructure to identify and quantify both benefits and costs incurred by the data holder and the data-seeking organization. Identification of the potential benefits of expanded data access and use will also be important for building public support for these activities. To build public support effectively, the panel recommends that operations within a new data infrastructure be transparent regarding tangible benefits and costs/risks incurred.

> Data sharing is incentivized when all data holders enjoy tangible benefits valuable to their missions, and when societal benefits are proportionate to possible costs and risks. (Conclusion 3-2)

Attribute 4: Reformed Legal Authorities Protecting All Parties' Interests

In the panel's judgment, a new data infrastructure needs to rest on a legal and regulatory framework that clearly defines which data assets can be shared, with whom, and for what purposes. The current infrastructure is far from the ideal described earlier. The U.S. statistical system is decentralized and governed by multiple statutes. There is no single legal framework controlling access and use of government data assets. For data-acquiring federal agencies, agency authorities determine the requirements and protections that govern the use of a given data asset. In some cases, statutes explicitly address access and use while, in other cases, agencies interpret their statutory authority to implicitly permit data sharing or access by external actors.[4] Clearly, legislative and regulatory changes are needed to support expanded data access with strengthened privacy protections.

In terms of access to federal data, the Evidence Act represents a major advance. First, the act made confidentiality requirements more consistent across statistical agencies and units and strengthened confidentiality requirements for many others. The act gave the director of OMB authority to designate agencies or organizational units as statistical agencies (U.S. Congress, 2019, Section 3562). Second, the act directed that federal-program and administrative-agency data assets be shared with statistical agencies unless explicitly prohibited by law. This expanded statistical agencies' access to the data of some federal administrative agencies, for statistical purposes (U.S. Congress, 2019, Section 3581), and permitted federal statistical agencies to share their own statistical data with each other. The act also expanded secure

---

[4]IRS Title 26, 6103(j) is an example of an explicit statute limiting access to tax data with explicit exceptions, while the U.S. Department of Agriculture has interpreted its statutory authority to implicitly permit the sharing of Supplemental Nutrition Assitance Program data for statistical purposes. See: https://uscode.house.gov/quicksearch/get.plx?title=26&section=6103

access to CIPSEA data for statistical purposes, including evidence building, to the extent practicable and unless prohibited by law (U.S. Congress, 2019, Section 3582). Unfortunately, at this writing, the director of OMB has not issued related rules and regulations to advance data sharing among statistical agencies.

However, there are many valuable government data assets whose use for statistical purposes is limited. For example, the Evidence Act's CIPSEA 2018 amendment (Evidence Act, Part B) did not revise Internal Revenue Service regulation 6103(j) to permit the U.S. Census Bureau to share limited business tax data with the Bureau of Labor Statistics (BLS) and the Bureau of Economic Analysis. State-collected and maintained high-value administrative data assets, including those associated with federally funded programs, also have statutory restrictions on access and use.

The Evidence Act addressed only federal data. The web of legal and regulatory limitations on state and local government data assets is even more complex than the federal framework. State laws may impose restrictions and obligations on businesses and institutions relating to the collection, use, and disclosure of information about its residents. Recently, some states (e.g., California, Virginia, and Colorado) have enacted comprehensive consumer privacy and protection laws.[5] New York has enacted the Stop Hacks and Improve Electronic Data Security (SHIELD) Act, which amended the existing data-breech notification law and imposed additional data-security requirements on companies.[6] According to the International Comparative Legal Guides, some 20 other states are considering comprehensive privacy laws.[7] As the privacy landscape continues to evolve, the panel advises that a new data infrastructure be responsive to these changes.

Even in the absence of prohibitive state laws, gaining access to state administrative data can be a time-consuming and daunting task that may not provide information in a timely enough manner to prevent collective harm following natural disasters or other shocks. For example, the creation of the Longitudinal Employer Household Dynamics program,[8] which combines administrative data on business establishments and workers with household- and business survey based data, took more than a decade to implement and still relies on scores of individual memoranda of understanding (MOUs) that must be regularly renegotiated with individual states.

Federal data-privacy laws also limit which federal data can be shared.

---

[5]See: California Consumer Privacy Act, https://leginfo.legislature.ca.gov/faces/codes_displayText.xhtml?division=3.&part=4.&lawCode=CIV&title=1.81.5; Virginia Consumer Data Protection Act: https://lis.virginia.gov/cgibin/legp604.exe?211+sum+SB1392; Colorado Privacy Act: https://leg.colorado.gov/sites/default/files/2021a_190_signed.pdf
[6]See: https://ag.ny.gov/internet/data-breach
[7]See: https://iclg.com/practice-areas/data-protection-laws-and-regulations/usa
[8]See: https://lehd.ces.census.gov/

The Privacy Act of 1974 covers federal agencies and the records they control (U.S. Congress, 1974). In terms of private sector data assets, laws govern data privacy and protection as well as the collection of information online. Several sector-specific federal laws govern data privacy and use (Osano, 2020). For example, the Health Insurance Portability and Accountability Act (HIPAA) governs the collection of health information. The Gramm Leach Billey Act governs personal information collected by banks and financial institutions. The Fair Credit Reporting Act regulates the collection and use of credit information. The Family Educational Rights and Privacy Act (FERPA) protects the confidentiality of student education records. Most of these laws permit limited research and statistical uses. Standardizing procedures for research and statistical use of data would aid the functioning of a new data infrastructure.

By contrast, private sector data brokers collect, buy, aggregate, and sell data on individuals and companies for profit, with few legal restrictions. The largest data brokers include Acxiom LLC, Epsilon Data Management LLC, Equifax, Experian, and CoreLogic (Privacy Bee, 2021). Consumers (the data subjects) are often unaware of data brokers' existence or practices. Consumers generally do not provide express permission or consent for use of their data by data brokers. Data brokers are almost entirely unregulated; there is no federal law regulating businesses that buy and sell personal information, and businesses face few penalties for causing harm to data subjects. However, two states, Vermont and California, have enacted data-broker laws.[9]

The growth of crowdsourced and citizen-science data has also raised concerns about data privacy and data protection (Eticas Foundation, 2020). When the public is enlisted to collect and/or share data, there is substantial variation in the level and quality of training they receive about such issues as harm mitigation, confidentiality, or ethical uses of data.

Inadequate protection for the autonomy of statistical agencies is another concern. Citro et al. (2022) provide three main findings regarding the autonomy of principle statistical agencies:

1. The challenges faced by statistical agencies arise largely as a consequence of insufficient autonomy.
2. There is remarkable variation in autonomy protections and a surprising lack of statutory protections for many agencies for many of the proposed measures. Only four statistical agencies have agency-specific autonomy protections. The remaining nine agencies are protected in varying degrees by blanket provisions, MOUs, or other defenses.

---

[9]See: https://www.classlawgroup.com/consumer-protection/privacy/data-brokers/

3. Many existing autonomy rules and guidelines are weakened by unclear or unactionable language (Citro et al., 2022, pp. 2–3).

Finally, the panel is not aware of any laws or regulations that prohibit companies or individuals who are not sworn agents of statistical agencies from profiting from information that they provide to statistical agencies. For example, in the panel's opinion, it will be important for data-sharing arrangements to prohibit parties from financial trading in advance of statistical releases, based on private information those parties provided to statistical agencies. Similarly, arrangements must also prohibit intentional manipulation of shared information to bias official statistics for any purpose.

In short, it is the panel's opinion that the current legal and regulatory framework that limits which data assets can be shared, with whom, and for what purposes does not satisfy the demands of a modern data infrastructure. The current framework prohibits beneficial sharing and lacks consistent requirements to preserve privacy, protect confidentiality, assure autonomy, and prevent abuse of data-sharing arrangements. Thus, legislative reform is needed.

Legislative and Regulatory Reform Is Required for a 21st Century Data Infrastructure

The Evidence Act is a major advance in promoting data access and use, but the full promise of the Commission on Evidence-based Policymaking (CEP) is yet to be achieved. In its deliberations about the implications of the Evidence Act, the Advisory Committee on Data for Evidence Building (ACDEB) suggested legislative actions be taken as soon as possible to promote expanded data access and use (Box 3-5). The panel assumes that, in its vision of a new data infrastructure, such steps will be taken successfully so that additional access to private sector data can occur.

Legal and regulatory changes are necessary to achieve the full promise of a 21st century national data infrastructure. (Conclusion 3-3)

Attribute 5: Governance Framework and Standards Effectively Supporting Operations

In the panel's view, the legal reform needed to underlie a new data infrastructure must be accompanied by a set of practices and policies consistent with the spirit of those new laws. "Data governance" refers to a framework of protocols that guide such practices—it is much more than a

---

BOX 3-5
Advisory Committee on Data for Evidence Building
Recommendations for Regulatory Action (Year 1 Report)

1. The OMB (Office of Management and Budget) director should take immediate steps to promulgate draft guidance and regulations required under the Foundations for Evidence-Based Policymaking Act. Expected policies include:
   - Notice of Proposed Rulemaking under CIPSEA (Confidential Information Protection and Statistical Efficiency Act) Section 3581, providing statistical agencies with the presumption of accessibility to federal program and administrative data assets.
   - Notice of Proposed Rulemaking under CIPSEA Section 3582, expanding access to CIPSEA data assets, including data-sensitivity considerations.
   - Notice of Proposed Rulemaking under CIPSEA Section 3563, on responsibilities for statistical agencies and public trust.
2. The OMB director should develop legislative proposals for Congress or regulatory actions to consider in implementing the remaining Evidence Commission recommendations recommended by the ACDEB, including:
   - Recommendation 2-6, encouraging expanded access to quarterly earnings and income data already acquired by federal agencies.
   - Using legislation to expand access to the National Directory of New Hires.

SOURCE: Advisory Committee on Data for Evidence Building (2021), pp. 9 and 18.

---

process. Some frameworks define data governance as "the ability to manage the life cycle of data through the implementation of policies, processes and rules in accordance with the organisation's strategic objectives."[10]

For discussion purposes, the panel defines the data-governance framework as including the authorities; structures; roles and responsibilities; policies, rules, and directives; guiding principles; and resources needed to support a new data infrastructure. Key data infrastructure capabilities include acquiring, accessing, using, managing, and protecting data assets. Data governance thus involves organizations, people, processes, policies, and technologies. It is ideally characterized by active stakeholder engagement; open and transparent communication; clear rules, procedures, and mechanisms; accountability; and oversight (British Academy and the Royal Society, 2017).

In the panel's judgment, data governance is crucial and must address the blending of multiple data sources, the need to respect the interests and

---

[10]See Common Statistical Data Architecture Capabilities: https://statswiki.unece.org/download/attachments/129177312/HLG-MOS%20Reference%20Data%20Architecture%20v1.0.docx?version=1&modificationDate=1516727545541&api=v2

rights of data subjects, and changing notions of privacy and consent. Blending survey data with new data sources, like private sector data, may raise additional ethical issues that warrant study. Governance must achieve more equitable data use in the face of a widening data divide, and it must recognize that risks and benefits associated with data use vary depending on the context and the purpose for which data are being used. Finally, governance must manage the burden imposed on data subjects and data holders, and be alert to the ever-present risk of a public data-related controversy (British Academy and the Royal Society, 2017).

The panel examined the evolving discussion surrounding data governance in the U.S. and governance protocols emerging from other countries. The principles underlying the governance framework necessary for a new data infrastructure are precisely those articulated in the panel's vision—deep devotion to privacy-protecting mechanisms, respect for data holders' and data subjects' interests and rights, and the provision of tangible benefits to those who share data for blending to produce improved information on critical societal features.

Components of data governance guide decisions for acquiring, sharing, using, managing, safeguarding, and stewarding data. The governance framework shapes important data-governance components, as shown in Box 3-6.[11] Many of these data-governance components require the active engagement of the diverse stakeholders (data subjects, data holders, and responsible organizations) within a data infrastructure. Such involvement is of growing prevalence (British Academy and the Royal Society, 2017) and is a central feature of both the U.K. Data Strategy (U.K. Department for Digital, Culture, Media & Sport, 2019) and the European Data Strategy (European Commission, n.d.).

Data-Governance Questions

While the National Academies' December 2021 workshops on The Scope, Components, and Key Characteristics of a 21st Century Data Infrastructure touched on data governance, they did not focus on specific data-governance requirements. Faced with an evolving data ecosystem across the nation and the world, the panel advises that the governance framework for a new data infrastructure be adaptable, grounded in fundamental principles, and able to recognize and address possible tensions between increasing data use and the possible risks of that use.

At this stage of its evolution, much of the governance framework of a new data infrastructure must remain unspecified. The nature of the

---

[11]See: https://unece.org/sites/default/files/2021-11/HLG2021_D1_ProjectProposal%20 Statistical%20Data%20Governance%20Framework.pdf

---

BOX 3-6
Data Governance Components

- Data governance bodies and structures. The structures often focus on various aspects of governance: strategic, tactical, and operational.
- Necessary authorities to access, link, and use data.
- Standards and guidance to facilitate interoperability, uniformity, and reuse.
- Policies, rules, and procedures that govern data acquisition, access, use, management, and protection.
- Processes and capabilities that touch data, like data exchange and data transformation.
- Platforms, technologies, and tools to access data from diverse platforms, perform necessary linkages, and conduct analysis while preserving privacy and protecting confidentiality.

SOURCE: Panel generated.

---

governance framework will depend upon both the passage of necessary legal reforms and the organizational structures chosen to implement the governance procedures. However, certain key questions *can* be identified now. The panel recommends consideration of the following questions to aid development of an effective, comprehensive, and responsive data-governance framework for a new data infrastructure:

1. What data-governance authorities are needed? Authority for overall governance of a new data infrastructure needs to be clarified, along with possible authority needed by any oversight body.
   - Who makes the decision to permit statistical uses of multiple data sources?
   - Who can impose sanctions for violations of data-use agreements?
   - Who ensures that data are properly documented?
2. What form of governance oversight is needed over the full data infrastructure? The National Academies recommends a board of directors (the National Academies, 2017a); CEP recommends a steering committee that includes representatives of the public, federal departments, state agencies, and academia (Commission on Evidence-Based Policymaking, 2017). Questions remain:
   - Is the board or steering committee simply advisory, or does it have specific authority?
   - How does the board or steering committee composition reflect the appropriate multistakeholder diversity?

3. What accountability mechanisms are needed to ensure compliance with laws, policies, and standards and to ensure ethical practices related to data management, data use, and data users? The Federal Data Ethics Framework tenet states:

> Accountability requires that anyone acquiring, managing, or using data be aware of stakeholders and be responsible to them, as appropriate. Remaining accountable includes the responsible handling of classified and controlled information, upholding data use agreements made with data providers [data holders], minimizing data collection, informing individuals and organizations of the potential uses of their data, and allowing for public access, amendment, and contestability to data and findings, where appropriate (Federal Data Strategy, n.d., p. 4).

Questions include:
- What accountability mechanisms need to be established?
- How will the system provide remedy and redress?

Standards: An Important Component of Data Governance

Just as data governance implements the spirit of legal reform permitting a new data infrastructure, "standards" are the logical implementations for some features of data governance and are important building blocks for a new data infrastructure. Standards facilitate the acquisition, collection, and organization of data, but also support other important data-infrastructure capabilities, such as blending of data.

Useful data sharing requires interoperability. Data have to be exchanged across users and should be comparable over time, space, and subpopulations. For example, interoperability in healthcare means separate systems, devices, organizations, and entities can exchange and appropriately use health-related data. Comparability means the unemployment rate in Los Angeles should have the same meaning as that in rural West Virginia. The unemployment rate in March 2022 should have the same interpretation as the unemployment rate in January 2018. Unemployment among those 18–25 years old should mean the same as unemployment among those 45–60 years old. Interoperability and comparability rest on the consistent application of standards for data elements, classification schemes, documentation, time periods, and more.

The interoperable exchange of multiple data sources starts with data documentation, commonly referred to as metadata. Metadata require the use of standards, especially for data documentation. Statistical surveys have relied on standard, consistent questions and definitions to collect information from individuals, households, establishments, or enterprises. The panel recognizes that survey participants may not recall or retain the requested information, business records may not align with the concept a survey is attempting to measure, or survey participants may not read the instructions or understand the questions. Yet, survey questions developed by statistical agencies or their contractors have been tested, the recordkeeping practices of businesses are periodically assessed,[12] and statistical data assets commonly contain associated metadata. The situation for other data-holder data assets may be quite different, but standards are critical if data are to be exchanged and used for statistical purposes. Lack of standards is one of the biggest obstacles to using health data, for example (Moyer, 2021).

Central governments often encourage the use of statistical standards to ensure the usefulness of statistical information. Statistical standards result in the production and publication of consistent, comparable information. In the United States, for example, there are standard definitions of metropolitan areas, of occupations, of industries and products, and basic units of measurement (e.g., length, width, weight). These standards, when accepted by populations, become an integral part of how businesses compare one another, how institutions assess their size, and how households assess their welfare. As Katherine Wallman, workshop participant, noted, data standards also can be an important gift to data holders and can incentivize them to share their data. Standards permit the coordination of actors on shared documentation, and, in return, government statistical agencies can use standardized data to report back to stakeholders, creating a virtuous cycle of standards and information useful to society.

In the panel's judgment, a new data infrastructure needs to adopt existing data standards, when appropriate, and promote the creation of new standards. Standardizing the definitions of the top 25 health data elements should be a priority, for example, as noted by workshop participant Niall Brennan. Shared standards are key to measuring data quality. Coverage, for example, depends on a shared understanding of the total data universe. Given that different data sources represent different segments of a universe (e.g., only businesses with paid employees) or even different universes (e.g., households vs. businesses), understanding coverage is an essential part of ensuring that a new data infrastructure benefits all.

No single data standard exists or is possible. Appendix 3B contains a partial listing of many alternative data-exchange and metadata standards, including global consortia of organizations seeking to increase the interoperability of data. The partial list demonstrates the existence of standards across diverse sectors of data. There are many standards-developing organizations and, consequently, many distinct standards. At the federal level, "adopting standards is a means by which the separate U.S. federal statistical

---

[12]See: https://play.google.com/books/reader?id=QzODHZLU9Z0C&pg=GBS.PA18&hl=en

agencies can achieve some uniformity and interoperability among their data and metadata systems in terms of both data stores and services" (the National Academies, 2021, p. 116). It is important to note that the most effective standards are created with ongoing input from stakeholders—stakeholders are the implementers of the standards and thus must realize benefits from them.

Matthew Gee discussed the use-cases that were primary drivers of a public-private effort to create uniform interoperable standards for jobs and employment records kept by employers (Gee, 2021). Ivan Deloatch, workshop participant, discussed the use-cases that were primary drivers for a public-private effort to create uniform interoperable standards for jobs and employment records kept by employers (Gee, 2021). Ivan Deloatch, Federal Geographic Data Committee, shared the experiences of the multi-agency geospatial community in defining standards and interoperability over a complex landscape of data collection and use.[13] In short, a modern data infrastructure resting on more data sharing would be greatly advanced by the adoption of common standards across the partners.

> **Effective data governance is critical and should be inclusive and accountable; governance policies and standards facilitating interoperability include key stakeholders and oversight bodies. (Conclusion 3-4)**

Attribute 6: Transparency to the Public Regarding Analytical Operations Using the Infrastructure

In addition to the attributes described above, the panel believes that transparency is critical to building the trust essential to engendering widespread support for a new data infrastructure.[14] A new data infrastructure, in the panel's view, must be viewed as legitimate by the participating data holders, data subjects, and society at large. A new infrastructure will include more sources of data from more data holders on more data subjects than did the data infrastructure of the 20th century. To be useful indicators of the country's welfare, the statistical information derived from a new data infrastructure must be credible and trusted. Transparency is critical, and "those engaged in generating and using data and evidence should operate transparently, providing meaningful channels for public input and comment and ensuring that evidence produced is made publicly available" (Commission on Evidence-Based Policymaking, 2017, p. 17).

---

[13]See: https://www.fcdc.gov/standards/fgdc-standards-program-overview

[14]For a more in-depth discussion of the importance of transparency in official statistics, see the National Academies (2022a, pp. 35–38).

Therefore, in the panel's opinion, transparency must be a stated requisite in the legal basis of a new data infrastructure, as well as part of that infrastructure's data-governance framework. Formal governance roles can be designed to enhance transparency. Transparency is also a prerequisite for accountability, which enables the public to express concerns, seek redress, and oversee compliance with the infrastructure's stated mission. For example, Organisation for Economic Co-operation and Development (OECD) member countries have passed legislation identifying individuals or institutions responsible for overseeing access to and dissemination of data in their respective countries:

- An ombudsman or mediator (e.g., in New Zealand, Norway, and Sweden);
- An information commissioner (e.g., in Germany, Hungary, Scotland, Slovenia, and the United Kingdom [U.K.]);
- A commission or institution (e.g., in Chile, France, Italy, Mexico, and Portugal);
- Another body responsible for monitoring this right, such as the Right to Information Assessment Review Council and the ombudsman in Turkey, both of which ensure the observance of all relevant laws (OECD, 2019, p. 15).

In the United Kingdom, establishment of the Statistics Authority was an attempt to achieve such visible oversight. As stated on the Authority's website:

The Authority is an independent statutory body. It operates at arm's length from government as a non-ministerial department and reports directly to the U.K. Parliament, the Scottish Parliament, the National Assembly for Wales and the Northern Ireland Assembly. The work of the Authority is further defined under secondary legislation made under the Act by the U.K. Parliament or the devolved legislatures.

The Authority has a statutory objective of promoting and safeguarding the production and publication of official statistics that 'serve the public good.' The public good includes:
- informing the public about social and economic matters; and
- assisting in the development and evaluation of public policy; and
- regulating quality and publicly challenging the misuse of statistics (U.K. Statistics Authority, 2022a).

The panel notes that the current United States legal and governance framework does not supply the level of transparency that these formal entities are promulgating.

The panel is cognizant of how tools of transparency have historically been manipulated to undermine trust in institutions, data, and science

(Pozen, 2018). Transparency alone cannot ensure that the public trusts a new data infrastructure, but a new data infrastructure cannot be trusted without transparency. Therefore, in the panel's opinion, transparency cannot be an end goal, but must be a commitment to iteratively engage with stakeholders to ensure an effective flow of information.

In sum, the panel advises that a 21st century national data infrastructure should seek the active engagement of diverse communities of interest, advocates of privacy protection, proponents of the benefits of broader data sharing, those concerned about data equity, and those promoting new national statistics. Multistakeholder participation is needed, and data holders must be represented and given a voice in making decisions that affect them, as well as in developing standards and establishing policies. At any time, the public, data holders, and data subjects should be able to know how their data are being used, by whom, for what purposes, and to what societal benefit. Transparent communication with the public, data holders, data subjects, and all relevant constituencies about how data are used and protected and how they are benefiting society can help instill confidence in a new data infrastructure and eventually result in societal trust in and "ownership" of that infrastructure.

> Trust in a new data infrastructure requires transparency of operations and accountability of the operators, with ongoing engagement of stakeholders. (Conclusion 3-5)

Attribute 7: State-of-the-Art Practices for Access, Statistical, Coordination, and Computational Activities; Continuously Improved to Efficiently Create Increasingly Secure and Useful Information

The panel notes that the skills required to support research and statistical operations on infrastructure data blended from diverse sources (see Chapter 4) include a combination of knowledge about network features, cybersecurity, secure multiparty computing, encryption, and other fields. These are new skills for many social and economic scientists who have, for decades, developed tools for measurement, data collection, data curation, data storage, and statistical disclosure analysis.

In the panel's judgment, the access and use of diverse data assets held by distinct data holders in various sectors will involve new partners who have divergent experiences with digital data. Data-seeking organizations will require expertise in working with data holders to understand the basic processes generating their data. Data-seeking organizations will need to discern which metadata standards are best suited to the data-holder organization, and they will need to understand and adapt to the data standards of the data holder. Data-seeking organizations will need to develop new frameworks for evaluating and communicating uncertainty and error in data. They may need to use stronger cybersecurity and privacy-protecting data curation. They must address the legal and procedural questions that the data holder will ask when initially considering sharing data assets. The panel expects that these skills need to evolve over time and that a new infrastructure should account for the dynamic nature of the digital society.

On the computational and statistical side, the panel believes that the data-seeker must have the talent to blend data together for more insightful research and statistical products. For example, pilot research projects have led to a new vision of how data might be shared between companies and statistical agencies in the 21st century (Haltiwanger et al., 2021). Because data holdings are so large that they cannot be transported from the data holder to the data-seeking statistical agency, active work is focusing on how data can be usefully and safely accessed and processed where they currently reside (i.e., at the data holder's facility). Software residing in the data holder's domain is being designed to fully comply with the data holder's user agreements. Software is designed to act on the data holder's existing data to produce aggregates that serve as the statistical building blocks that a federal statistical agency might use directly or blend with other survey or census data. Developing mechanisms to interoperate across distributed data sources will be key to a new data infrastructure, according to the panel's vision.

In the panel's opinion, such projects suggest that a new data infrastructure should have a novel, distributed design, with pre-vetted, safe software embedded behind the firewalls of both the data-seeking and data-holding organizations. Software, written collaboratively by both parties, would create pre-specified aggregates of data as described above. At a data holder's site, the software would produce, for the data seeker, new statistical products or intermediate inputs into other products. Existing and new products would be provided simultaneously to both the data holder and to the public. These new products could include benchmarks for data holders as well as detailed analyses of the performance of an economic sector (e.g., the changes in product diversity over time in an industry) while not undermining competition within an industry or sector.

As mentioned in Chapter 2, such pilot projects are now ongoing in federal statistical agencies, and the panel expects that important lessons will be learned. Like the Committee for National Statistics' report, *Federal Statistics, Multiple Data Sources, and Privacy Protection: Next Steps* (the National Academies, 2017a), the panel notes that computational approaches are likely to evolve over time, as innovation in computational and statistical methods for blended data continue. The sustainability of a new national data infrastructure requires practices that closely track these innovations and adapt to incorporate new technologies, methods, and capabilities.

While new technologies and advanced methods may offer significant benefits, they may also increase bias or inequity, so attention must be paid to ethical use of these innovations (Federal Data Strategy, n.d.). Smaller organizations and less-resourced data users may find running such pilots and adopting and maintaining new technologies to be difficult, which presents another practical challenge. Many likely lack the economies of scale and scope to employ highly skilled technologists and to purchase advanced software and hardware. Sharing services with a host organization may not be a solution if the organizations do not have similar needs, and sharing may be risky if it diminishes the autonomy of a statistical agency.

The operations of a new data infrastructure would benefit from the inclusion of continually evolving practices, methods, technologies, and skills, to ethically leverage new technologies and advanced methods. (Conclusion 3-6)

SUMMARY

This chapter has described a vision for a 21st century national data infrastructure along with seven key attributes that are listed in Box 3-2. Achieving the vision of a new data infrastructure with these attributes will not be easy, but it can be done. This chapter has identified important changes that are needed to achieve the requisite attributes, to make the vision of a 21st century national data infrastructure a reality. In the panel's judgment, commitment and action are required to fully realize the promise of this new infrastructure.

APPENDIX 3A:
LAWS AND OFFICE OF MANAGEMENT AND BUDGET GUIDANCE ON CONFIDENTIALITY AND PRIVACY PROTECTION[15]

Protecting the confidentiality of individual information collected under a confidentiality pledge—whether from individuals, households, businesses, or other organizations—is a bedrock principle of federal statistics. Federal statistical agencies also strive to respect the privacy of individual respondents through such means as limiting the collection of information to that which is necessary for an agency's mission. Respect for privacy has a history in federal legislation and regulation that extends back many decades; so, too, does protection of confidentiality, except that not all federal agencies were covered.[16] With the original passage of CIPSEA in 2002 (see below), a firm legislative foundation was established for confidentiality protection of statistical data governmentwide.

Privacy Act of 1974

The Privacy Act of 1974 (P.L. 93-579, as amended; codified at 5 USC 552a) is a landmark piece of legislation that grew out of concerns about the implications of computers, credit bureaus, proposals for national databanks, and the like on personal privacy. The act states in part (5 USC 552a(b)):

No agency shall disclose any record which is contained in a system of records by any means of communication to any person, or to another agency, except pursuant to a written request by, or with the prior written consent of, the individual to whom the record pertains, unless disclosure of the record [is subject to one or more of 12 listed conditions].

The defined conditions for disclosure of personal records without prior consent include use for statistical purposes by the Census Bureau, for statistical research or reporting when the records are to be transferred in a form that is not individually identifiable for routine uses within a U.S. government agency, for preservation by the National Archives and Records Administration "as a record which has sufficient historical or other value to warrant its continued preservation by the United States Government," for

---

[15]Excerpted from the National Academies (2021), pp. 159–168. Citations in this section are from the original text and are not included in this report's Reference list. See orignal text at https://nap.nationalacademies.org/catalog/24810 for complete details.

[16]For example, Title 13 of the U.S. Code, providing for confidentiality protection for economic and population data collected by the U.S. Census Bureau, dates back to 1929; in contrast, the Bureau of Labor Statistics had no legal authority for its policies and practices of confidentiality protection until the passage of CIPSEA in 2002 (see NRC, 2003, pp. 119–121).

law enforcement purposes, for congressional investigations, and for other administrative purposes.

The Privacy Act mandates that every federal agency have in place an administrative and physical security system to prevent the unauthorized release of personal records; it also mandates that every agency publish in the *Federal Register* one or more system of records notices (SORNs) for newly created and revised systems of records that contain personally identifiable information as directed by OMB.[17] SORNs are to describe not only the records and their uses by the agency, but also procedures for storing, retrieving, accessing, retaining, and disposing of records in the system.[18]

Federal Policy for the Protection of Human Subjects, 45 Code of Federal Regulations (CFR) 46, Subpart A ("Common Rule"), as Revised in 2017

The 1991 Common Rule regulations, promulgated by the U.S. Department of Health and Human Services (DHHS)[19] and signed onto by nine other cabinet departments and seven independent agencies (in their own regulations), represent the culmination of a series of DHHS regulations dating back to the 1960s (see Practice 7 and NRC, 2003, Ch. 3). The regulations are designed to protect individuals whom researchers wish to recruit for research studies funded by the federal government, which include surveys and other kinds of statistical data collection.[20]

These regulations require that researchers obtain informed consent from prospective participants, minimize risks to participants, balance risks and benefits appropriately, select participants equitably, monitor data collection to ensure participant safety (where appropriate), and protect participant privacy and maintain data confidentiality (where appropriate). Institutional Review Boards (IRBs) at universities and other organizations and agencies registered with DHHS review research protocols to determine whether they qualify for exemption from or are subject to IRB review and, if the latter, whether the protocol satisfactorily adheres to the regulations. Some federal statistical agencies are required to submit data-collection protocols to an IRB for approval; other agencies maintain exemption from IRB review but follow the principles and spirit of the regulations.

---

[17] See Office of Management and Budget (2016).

[18] For an example of SORNs for a statistical agency, see https://www.census.gov/about/policies/privacy/sorn.html [February 2021]

[19] See: https://www.hhs.gov/ohrp/regulations-and-policy/regulations/common-rule/ (February 2021). In addition to Subpart A of 45 CFR 46, DHHS and some other departments and agencies have signed onto Subparts B, C, and D, which pertain to pregnant women, human fetuses, and neonates; prisoners; and children, respectively.

[20] Of those departments with statistical units, all signed onto the Common Rule with the exception of the Departments of Labor and the Treasury.

An Advance Notice of Proposed Rulemaking, issued in 2011, proposed changes to the Common Rule, including revisions to the provisions for confidentiality protection.[21] A Notice of Proposed Rulemaking, which indicated responses to the extensive comments on that advance notice, was issued in 2015; it too included a comment period.[22] A final rule was published January 19th, 2017,[23] which took effect on January 19th, 2018 (for cooperative research involving more than one institution, the effective date was January 20th, 2020). Some of the changes from the 1991 version of the Common Rule are these:

- The U.S. Department of Labor became a signatory to the Common Rule; consequently, only one department that houses a federal statistical agency (U.S. Department of the Treasury) is not a signatory.
- Provisions to exempt research with human participants from IRB review were modified and enlarged and, where appropriate, IRB review is to be focused on the adequacy of confidentiality protection.
- To assist IRBs in determining the adequacy of confidentiality protection, the Secretary of DHHS, after consultation with OMB and other federal signatories, is to issue guidance on what provisions are adequate to protect the privacy of subjects and to maintain the confidentiality of data.
- Provisions are added for "broad" consent for storage, maintenance, and secondary research use of identifiable private information or biospecimens.

1997 Order Providing for the Confidentiality of Statistical Information

OMB issued this order in 1997 to bolster the confidentiality protections afforded by statistical agencies or unit (as listed in the order), some of which lacked legal authority to back up their confidentiality protection.[24] CIPSEA (see next section) placed confidentiality protection for statistical information on a strong legal footing across the entire federal government.

---

[21] See 76 Federal Register 44512 (July 26th, 2011). Available: https://www.federalregister.gov/d/2011-18792. See also NRC (2014).

[22] See 80 Federal Register 53933 (September 8th, 2015). Available: https://www.federalregister.gov/d/2015-21756

[23] See 82 Federal Register 7149 (January 19th, 2017). Available: https://www.federalregister.gov/d/2017-01058

[24] See 62 Federal Register 35044 (June 27th, 1997). Available: https://www.federalregister.gov/d/97-16934

Confidential Information Protection and Statistical Efficiency Act

The Confidential Information Protection and Statistical Efficiency Act (CIPSEA) was first enacted as Title V of the E-Government Act of 2002 (P.L. 107-347) and was recodified as part of the Evidence-Based Policy-making Act of 2018 (see above). CIPSEA provides a strong statutory basis for the statistical system with regard to confidentiality protection and data sharing. CIPSEA has four parts: two original parts cover confidentiality (Part B) and data sharing (Part C; efficiency), respectively, while the other two parts include definitions and *Statistical Policy Directive No. 1* (Part A), and Access to Data for Evidence (Part D; see Evidence Act above).

Part B, Confidential Information Protection

Part B of CIPSEA strengthens and extends statutory confidentiality protection for all statistical data collections of the U.S. government. Prior to CIPSEA, such protection was governed by a patchwork of laws applicable to specific agencies, judicial opinions, and agencies' practices. For all data furnished by individuals or organizations to an agency under a pledge of confidentiality for exclusively statistical purposes, Subtitle A provides that the data will be used only for statistical purposes and will not be disclosed in identifiable form to anyone not authorized by the title. It makes the knowing and willful disclosure of confidential statistical data a class E felony, with fines up to $250,000 and imprisonment for up to five years.

Subtitle A pertains not only to surveys, but also to collections by a federal agency for statistical purposes from nonpublic administrative records (e.g., confidential state government agency records). Data covered under Subtitle A are not subject to release under a Freedom of Information Act request.

Part C, Statistical Efficiency

Part C of CIPSEA permits the BEA, the BLS, and the Census Bureau to share individually identifiable business data for statistical purposes. The subtitle has three main purposes: (1) to reduce respondent burden on businesses; (2) to improve the comparability and accuracy of federal economic statistics by permitting these three agencies to reconcile differences among sampling frames, business classifications, and business reporting; and (3) to increase understanding of the U.S. economy and improve the accuracy of key national indicators, such as the National Income and Product Accounts.

However, this part does not authorize any new sharing among BEA, BLS, and the Census Bureau of any individually identifiable tax return data that originate from the Internal Revenue Service (IRS). This limitation currently blocks some kinds of business-data sharing, such as those for sole proprietorships, which are important for improving the efficiency and quality of business-data collection by statistical agencies. For tax return information, data sharing is limited to a small number of items for specialied uses by a small number of specific agencies (under Title 26, Section 6103 of the U.S. Code, and associated Treasury Department regulations, as modified in the 1976 Tax Reform Act). The governing statute would have to be modified to extend sharing of tax return items to agencies not specified in the 1976 legislation. Although proposals for legislation to expand access to IRS information for limited statistical purposes have been discussed and developed through interagency discussions, they have not received necessary congressional approval.

CIPSEA Implementation Guidance

OMB originally released implementation guidance for CIPSEA in 2007 (U.S. Office of Management and Budget, 2007). The guidance covered such topics as the steps that agencies must take to protect confidential information; wording of confidentiality pledges in materials that are provided to respondents; steps that agencies must take to distinguish any data or information they collect for nonstatistical purposes and to provide proper notice to the public of such data; and ways in which agents (e.g., contractors, researchers) may be designated to use individually identifiable information for analysis and other statistical purposes and be held legally responsible for protecting the confidentiality of that information. Under the Evidence Act, OMB is charged with promulgating guidance for implementation of a process to designate statistical agencies and units.[25] A total of 16 agencies and units are currently so recognized (see Appendix B).

Privacy Impact Assessments Required Under the E-Government Act of 2002, Section 208

Section 208 of the E-Government Act of 2002 (P.L. 107-347) requires federal agencies to conduct a privacy impact assessment whenever an agency develops or obtains information technology that handles individually identifiable information or whenever the agency initiates a new collection of individually identifiable information.[26] The assessment is to be made publicly available and cover topics such as what information is being collected and why, with whom the information will be shared,

---

[25]44 USC 3562(a).

[26]Section 208 also mandates that OMB lead interagency efforts to improve federal information technology and use of the Internet for government services.

what provisions will be made for informed consent regarding data sharing, and how the information will be secured. Typically, privacy impact assessments cover not only privacy issues, but also confidentiality, integrity, and availability issues.[27] OMB was required to issue guidance for development of the assessments, which was done in a September 26th, 2003, memorandum (M-03-22) from the OMB director to the heads of executive agencies and departments.[28]

Section 208, together with Title III, FISMA (see below), and Title V, CIPSEA (see above), of the 2002 E-Government Act are the latest in a series of laws beginning with the Privacy Act of 1974, that govern access to individual records maintained by the federal government (see also Federal Cybersecurity Enhancement Act of 2015, below).

Federal Information Security Management Act of 2002

FISMA was enacted in 2002 as Title III of the E-Government Act of 2002 (U.S. Congress, 2002a) to bolster computer and network security in the federal government and affiliated parties (such as government contractors) by mandating yearly audits.

FISMA imposes a mandatory set of processes that must be followed for all information systems used or operated by a federal agency or by a contractor or other organization on behalf of a federal agency. These processes must follow a combination of Federal Information Processing Standards documents, the special publications issued by the National Institute of Standards and Technology (SP-800 series), and other legislation pertinent to federal information systems, such as the Privacy Act of 1974 and the Health Insurance Portability and Accountability Act of 1996.

The first step is to determine what constitutes the "information system" in question. There is no direct mapping of computers to an information system; rather, an information system can be a collection of individual computers put to a common purpose and managed by the same system owner. The next step is to determine the types of information in the system and categorize each according to the magnitude of harm that would result if the system suffered a compromise of confidentiality, integrity, or availability. Succeeding steps are to develop complete system documentation, conduct a risk assessment, put appropriate controls in place to minimize risk, and arrange for an assessment and certification of the adequacy of the controls.

---

[27]See, for example, the available privacy impact assessments prepared by the Census Bureau at https:// www.census.gov/about/policies/privacy/pia.html

[28]See: https://www.whitehouse.gov/wp-content/uploads/2017/11/203-M-03-22-OMB-Guidance-for-Implementing-the-Privacy-Provisions-of-the-E-Government-Act-of-2002-1.pdf

FISMA affects federal statistical agencies directly in that each agency must follow the FISMA procedures for its own information systems. In addition, some departments are taking the position that all information systems in a department constitute a single information system for the purposes of FISMA: those departments are taking steps to require that statistical agencies' information systems and personnel be incorporated into a centralized, department-wide system.

Federal Information Technology Acquisition Reform Act of 2014

The Federal Information Technology Acquisition Reform Act (FITARA) was enacted on December 19, 2014, to respond to such federal information technology (IT) challenges as duplicate IT spending among and within agencies, difficulty in understanding the cost and performance of IT investments, and inability to benchmark IT spending between federal and private-sector counterparts. FITARA has four major objectives: (1) strengthening the authority over and accountability for IT costs, performance, and security of agency chief information officers (CIOs); (2) aligning IT resources with agency missions and requirements; (3) enabling more effective planning for and execution of IT resources; and (4) providing transparency about IT resources across agencies and programs. It requires agencies (defined as cabinet departments and independent agencies) to pursue a strategy of consolidation of agency data centers, charges agency CIOs with the responsibility for implementing FITARA, and charges the U.S. Government Accountability Office with producing quarterly scorecards to assess how well agencies are meeting the FITARA objectives.

The director of OMB issued implementation guidance for FITARA, M-15-14, *Management and Oversight of Federal Information Technology*, on June 20th, 2015.[29] This memorandum explicitly stated that agencies must implement the FITARA guidance to ensure that information acquired under a pledge of confidentiality solely for statistical purposes is used exclusively for those purposes. It also provided a "Common Baseline for IT Management," which lays out FITARA responsibilities of CIOs and other agency officials, such as the chief financial officer and program officials. On May 4th, 2016, the federal CIO and the administrator of OIRA, both in OMB, jointly issued *Supplemental Guidance on the Implementation of M-15-14 "Management and Oversight of Federal Information Technology"—Applying FITARA Common Baseline to Statistical Agencies and Units* (U.S. Office of Management and Budget, 2016). This supplemental guidance posing questions for CIOs and other officials, including

---

[29]See: https://obamawhitehouse.archives.gov/sites/default/files/omb/memoranda/2015/m-15-14.pdf

statistical agency heads, to address when implementing FITARA for statistical agency programs. The questions refer to the fundamental responsibilities of federal statistical agencies outlined in *Statistical Policy Directive No. 1* (see above), which include confidentiality protection and meeting deadlines for key statistics.

Federal Cybersecurity Enhancement Act of 2015

The Federal Cybersecurity Enhancement Act of 2015 is Title II, Subpart B, of the Cybersecurity Act of 2015, which was attached as a rider to the Consolidated Appropriations Act of 2016, and so became law (P.L. 114- 113) when the appropriations bill was signed on December 18, 2015. The impetus for Title II, Subpart B, was the efforts of the U.S. Department of Homeland Security (DHS), dating back to 2003, to deploy systems for detection and prevention of intrusions ("hacking") into federal government information networks (see Latham and Watkins, 2016, p. 3). At of the end of 2015, this technology, known as EINSTEIN, covered only 45 percent of federal network access points. The act requires DHS to "make [EINSTEIN] available" to all federal agencies within one year, and thereafter requires all agencies to "apply and continue to utilize the capabilities" across their networks.

The technology, currently in version E3A, has been welcomed by federal statistical agencies, but agencies initially were concerned about a DHS interpretation of the act that would allow DHS staff to monitor traffic on agency networks and follow up on actual or likely intrusions. Such surveillance by DHS staff could lead to violations of agencies' pledges to protect the confidentiality of information provided by individual respondents for statistical purposes, which state that only statistical agency employees or sworn agents can see such information. Ultimately, DHS retained its surveillance authority, and statistical agencies modified their confidentiality pledges. As described in a *Federal Register* notice from the U.S. Census Bureau (other statistical agencies have issued similar notices).[30]

DHS and Federal statistical agencies, in cooperation withtheir parent departments, have developed a Memorandum of Agreement for the installation of Einstein 3A cybersecurity protection technology to monitor their Internet traffic and have incorporated an associated Addendum on Highly Sensitive Agency Information that provides additional protection and enhanced security handling of confidential statistical data. However, many current Title 13, U.S.C. and similar statistical confidentiality pledges

---

[30]Agency Information Collection Activities; Request for Comments; Revision of the Confidentiality Pledge Under Title 13 United States Code, Section 9, 81 Federal Register 94321 (December 23rd, 2016). Available: https://www.federalregister.gov/d/2016-30959

promise that respondents' data will be seen only by statistical agency personnel or their sworn agents. Since it is possible that DHS personnel could see some portion of those confidential data in the course of examining the suspicious Internet packets identified by Einstein 3A sensors, statistical agencies need to revise their confidentiality pledges to reflect this process change.

The BLS led an interagency research program to test revised wording with samples of respondents, and agencies revised their pledges accordingly. As an example, the Census Bureau's revised pledge, provided in 81 *Federal Register* 94321 (December 23rd, 2016; see footnote 30), states:

> The U.S. Census Bureau is required by law to protect your information. The Census Bureau is not permitted to publicly release your responses in a way that could identify you. Per the Federal Cybersecurity Enhancement Act of 2015, your data are protected from cybersecurity risksthrough screening of the systems that transmit your data.

APPENDIX 3B:
EXAMPLES OF STANDARDS THAT WOULD BE
USEFUL TO ANY NEW DATA INFRASTRUCTURE

- Statistical Data and Metadata eXchange (SDMX): Formatting multidimensional data and metadata into a framework for automated data exchange among organizations.[31]
- The United Nations Economic Commission for Europe family of standards: Generic Statistical Business Process Model (GSBPM; defines the set of business processes needed to produce official statistics), Generic Statistical Information Model (GSIM; a reference framework of internationally agreed-upon definitions, attributes, and relationships that describe the information objects used in the production of official statistics), Common Statistical Production Architecture (CSPA; a reference architecture for the statistics industry covering GSBPM processes and providing a link between GSIM and GSBPM), and Common Statistical Data Architecture (CSDA; provides a data-centric view of a statistical institute's architecture, putting a focus on data, metadata, and data capabilities needed to treat data as an asset).[32]
- The Data Documentation Initiative (DDI): An international standard that can document and manage specific stages in the research data lifecycle, such as conceptualization, collection, processing, distribution, discovery, and archiving.[33]
- The National Information Exchange Model (NIEM): A common vocabulary that enables efficient information exchange across diverse public and private organizations. The NIEM defines agreed-upon terms, definitions, relationships, and formats—independent of how information is stored in individual systems—for data being exchanged.[34]
- The International Organization for Standardization (ISO) and the International Electrotechnical Commission (IEC) 11179: Provides a conceptual model for managing classification schemes. There are many structures used to organize classification schemes, and there are many subject matter areas that classification schemes describe. So, ISO/IEC 11179 also provides a two-faceted classification for classification schemes themselves.[35]

---

[31] See: https://sdmx.org/
[32] See: https://unece.org/statistics/standards-and-metadata
[33] See: https://ddialliance.org/
[34] See: https://www.niem.gov
[35] See: https://www.iso.org/standard/60341.html

- International and domestic standards for electronic data interchanges: The predominant electronic data interchange standard in the U.S. is ANSI X12. The Securities and Exchange Commission uses XBRL for company financial reporting in EDGAR.[36]
- The Geospatial Data Act of 2018: This Act established the Federal Geographic Data Committee (FGDC) as the lead entity in the federal government for the development, implementation, and review of policies, practices, and standards relating to geospatial data. The FGDC has years of working with federal statistical, program, and administrative agencies to devise data standards related to collection, sharing, use, dissemination, and mitigation of risk.[37]

---

[36]See: https://x12.org/

[37]See: https://www.fgdc.gov/standards and also standards for metadata and interoperability: https://www.fgdc.gov/metadata; https://www.fgdc.gov/what-we-do/develop-geospatial-shared-services/interoperability/gira

4

Blended Data:
Implications for a New National Data
Infrastructure and Its Organization

In the panel's vision, a 21st century national data infrastructure should support blending data from multiple sources to provide accurate, timely, and relevant information. Blended data occur when at least two different data assets are combined to produce statistical information. This chapter describes diverse data assets that can be combined for statistical purposes; the criteria that govern data acquisition, access, and use; and the implications of blended data on the components and capabilities of a 21st century national data infrastructure, as well as the associated privacy and ethical challenges. The chapter ends with a consideration of various organizational structures that may facilitate cross-sector data access and use.

KEY DATA HOLDERS FOR A 21ST CENTURY
NATIONAL DATA INFRASTRUCTURE

As described in Chapter 2, statistical agencies are already blending data from multiple sources, consistent with the recommendations of several expert reports. This section describes the scope of data assets that the panel recommends being included in a new infrastructure as well as the holders of those data assets. Data holders include federal statistical agencies; federal program and administrative agencies; state, local, tribal, and territory governments; private sector companies including data brokers; nonprofits and academic institutions; and crowdsourced and citizen-science data holders.

Before describing data holders, a few words on data subjects. Respecting the presence and rights of data subjects—the people, entities, or organizations described by the data—is essential to building widespread trust in a new data infrastructure. Distinct types of data subjects require distinct kinds of considerations. First, data assets may relate to, describe, or be associated with an identified or identifiable individual, consumer, or household. Second, data may relate to, describe, or be associated with an identifiable business, including corporations, partnerships, limited liability companies, and sole proprietorships. Third, data assets may describe a physical structure including residential (single-family and multifamily), nonresidential, private, nonprofit, or government-owned structures. Fourth, data may relate to a specific process, system, or application. Web survey paradata (i.e., data that document the measurement process) are an example of process-related data that could also potentially identify a data subject. For example, an agency's paradata could relate to an individual, household, or business; or to a statistical agency's information about a portal, a survey, a web instrument, a question, a survey-specific item, information about the device used by a respondent, or the combination of any of the above. The concerns, interests, and special considerations needed to account for data subjects are covered in subsequent sections.

The data holders listed below have data assets relevant to the panel's vision of a new data infrastructure. The panel acknowledges that, individually, all data assets are likely to have weaknesses, but a careful blending of data from multiple complementary sources, such as statistical surveys and censuses, administrative agencies, and private sector enterprises, can emolliate the weaknesses of any single data source. Blending these multiple data sources offers new opportunities to generate more timely, granular, and useful statistics for the common good.

Principal Federal Statistical Agencies and Units

In the panel's vision of a new data infrastructure, the existing and future data assets of designated statistical agencies and units (as shown previously in Box 3-3) should be available for blending, subject to strong privacy protections and ethical considerations, with other data. Data assets would include identifiable and privacy-protected data files, metadata, and paradata "created by, collected by, under the control or direction of, or maintained" by the 13 principal statistical agencies and designated units (U.S. Congress, 2019).

The traditional data assets of statistical agencies have many desirable attributes. These data were designed to serve national statistical informational needs. They are derived from high-quality registers and sampling frames, have strong coverage properties, measure many attributes of the respondents, and use statistical methods to generate high-quality estimates. They have existing legal underpinnings vetted by U.S. Congress and the executive branch. However, as noted in Chapter 2, statistical surveys and censuses are slow to produce information, expensive, and suffer from declining participation.

Statistical agency data assets are also structured with a well-defined data model (i.e., the locations of attributes within data records are documented and described). For the purpose of the panel's vision, associated metadata should describe the data source, format, variables, data elements, questions, processes, methods, limitations, and more. Statistical agency data assets also include semi-structured paradata files (that describe details of the measurement process) and possibly unstructured data, such as text descriptions of property attributes in land property descriptions. Access to and use of statistical agency microdata files is generally restricted by law or regulation; privacy and confidentiality are legislatively protected (U.S. Congress, 1974, 2019).

Section 3582 of the Foundations for Evidence-Based Policymaking Act of 2018 (hereafter, Evidence Act) directs statistical agencies to share restricted, secure data assets with other statistical and nonstatistical agencies for purposes of evidence building unless restricted by law (U.S. Congress, 2019). The ability to share restricted data assets among statistical agencies represents an important new opportunity to improve and transform statistical programs and operations. The Evidence Act's sharing presumption of "yes, unless"[1] is an advance over prior regulation. However, as noted by Katherine Wallman, workshop participant, the "unless" can still be a huge obstacle.

Statistical data agency assets, of course, are not without problems. A lack of complete records, ambiguous questions, or poor recall among data subjects can contribute to underlying issues. In addition, self-identification and changes over time in the meanings of race and/or ethnicity,[2] gender, and industry or occupation can contribute to measurement challenges.

Federal Programs and Administrative Agencies

Program-based federal agencies (e.g., the U.S. Department of Agriculture's Supplemental Nutrition Assistance Program) possess data assets that could complement and extend existing statistical programs, generate new products, and expand data assets available to researchers. These data are often termed administrative data. Blending administrative data with data collected by statistical agencies is an active area of innovation in federal statistical agencies and in the research community.

The U.S. Census Bureau has been using federal tax data in the quinquennial economic censuses program since the mid-1950s, and in building

---

[1] If a statistical agency seeks a federal data asset *for statistical purposes*, the requested data must be provided unless specifically prohibited by law.

[2] For discussions of measurement implications, see Prewitt (2013) and Alba (2020).

its business register since the early 1970s. The National Academies of Sciences, Engineering, and Medicine discussed in detail the benefits and challenges of using government administrative data for federal statistics, and described the use of administrative data in other countries (the National Academies of Sciences, Engineering, and Medicine, 2017b, Ch. 3). That report noted the impressive added value of blending survey data with government-program data.

Without imposing additional reporting burden, government administrative data have been used to update business and address frames and to provide universe statistics, such as nonemployer statistics. These data have been used for editing and imputation of survey responses or missing items, as a source of auxiliary information in statistical models, for survey evaluation, and to guide data-collection efforts in the conduct of surveys and censuses. The 2020 decennial United States census used administrative data to guide the number of nonresponse follow-up contacts, to inform proxy responses for nonrespondents, and to check data quality. However, administrative data also have limitations—lack of quality control or quality measures, coverage limitations, missing records, concepts or definitions that may differ between statistical surveys, lack of timeliness, and high processing costs (Liao et al., 2020). Linking survey and administrative data sources can help identify such problems and lead to improvements in administrative data sources.

By statute, the U.S. Office of Management and Budget (OMB) requires agencies to look for alternative data sources before conducting a new survey.[3] However, despite the spirit of the Evidence Act's directive to expand use of existing data for statistical purposes, the Act does not override current statutory prohibitions regarding sharing. For example, the Internal Revenue Code 6103(j) regulations permit the U.S. Census Bureau to use tax data for a limited, specified set of purposes, but does not permit the Bureau to share tax data or survey data comingled with tax information with the Bureau of Labor Statistics (BLS) or the Bureau of Economic Analysis (BEA; U.S. Congress, 2022b), even though the 2002 Confidential Information Protection and Statistical Efficiency Act (CIPSEA; U.S. Congress, 2002b) permitted the sharing of business data among the three agencies. Consequently, the U.S. Census Bureau and BLS maintain separate business registers that are not reconciled, which complicates the blending of data assets and products across the agencies.

Data synchronization legislation was drafted to revise the Internal Revenue Service (IRS) regulation so that the U.S. Census Bureau could share limited business tax data with BLS and BEA. This legislation, while

---

[3]See 5 C.F.R.: 1320, https://www.govinfo.gov/app/details/CFR-2016-title5-vol3/CFR-2016-title5-vol3-part1320

BOX 4-1
Updated CEP Examples of Selected Administrative Data Assets

- Vital Statistics System (National Center for Health Statistics)
- Head Start Programs (U.S. Department of Health and Human Services)
- Children's Health Program (U.S. Department of Health and Human Services)
- Supplemental Nutrition and Assistance Program (U.S. Department of Agriculture)
- Federal Student Aid (U.S. Department of Education)
- Housing Assistance (U.S. Department of Housing and Urban Development)
- Federal Tax Data (Internal Revenue Service)
- Unemployment Insurance Quarterly Wage Records (federal/state)
- SBA Paycheck Protection Program
- Military and Veterans Programs (U.S. Department of Defense, U.S. Department of Veterans Affairs)
- Criminal Justice Data (Federal Bureau of Investigation, law enforcement agencies)
- Medicaid, Medicare, and Children's Health Program (U.S. Social Security Administration)
- Social Security Disability, Old Age and Survivors Insurance (U.S. Social Security Administration)
- National Directory of New Hires (U.S. Department of Health and Human Services)

SOURCE: Commission on Evidence-Based Policymaking, 2017, Appendix D.

---

proposed multiple times since 2002, has never been enacted,[4] foregoing a major opportunity to improve economic statistics and cut costs (American Economic Association, 2021).

In 2017, the Commission on Evidence-Based Policymaking (CEP) recognized the importance of administrate data as an additional data source for evidence-building (Commission on Evidence-Based Policymaking, 2017). Box 4-1 provides a "cradle-to-grave" listing of selected CEP administrative data sources, with the Small Business Administration (SBA's) Paycheck Protection Program[5] added.

The Evidence Act addressed a major barrier to data access by providing statistical agencies with a broader statutory basis for accessing and using data assets of other federal agencies (U.S. Congress, 2019, Section 3581)

---

[4]Legislation was pushed in in 2014, see *Federal Register* notice proposing a rule change to 6103(j)(1)(A): https://www.federalregister.gov/documents/2014/07/15/2014-16597/disclosures-of-return-information-reflected-on-returns-to-officers-and-employees-of-the-department

[5]For more information on the Paycheck Protection Program, see: https://www.sba.gov/funding-programs/loans/covid-19-relief-options/paycheck-protection-program/ppp-data

unless prohibited by statute. Yet, most of these administrative data assets remain untapped for use beyond their home agencies, and they are often unavailable by statute for statistical uses or research. This contrasts starkly with Statistics Canada, which has adopted an "administrative data first" policy (Statistics Canada, 2015).

State, Tribal, Territory, and Local Governments

State, tribal, territory, and local governments possess data assets that could help produce blended national statistics by facilitating more granular, sub-national statistics, thus enriching localities' understanding of their social and economic conditions. For example, local governments and cities are using data to make smarter, more informed decisions.[6] In the panel's vision, a new data infrastructure should include such state, tribal, territory, and local government data assets, creating blended statistics of greater value.

Provision of funding to states, tribal lands, local governments, and territories could incentivize such sharing by helping these data holders to use information, establishing two-way data sharing, and thus adding value for local decisionmaking (Moyer, 2021). Capacity building at the state and local levels, as suggested by the Advisory Committee on Data for Evidence Building (ACDEB), could make a significant impact on data quality, with benefits to both administration of state and local programs and the quality of national statistics (Advisory Committee on Data for Evidence Building, 2021).

For example, BLS funds states to clean and share their unemployment insurance employer records so that BLS can compile these administrative data into the Quarterly Census of Employment and Wages (QCEW). BLS uses this series to construct its Business Register, the universe frame for its current surveys of businesses. The QCEW is a by-product of the federal-state unemployment insurance partnership, supplemented by two BLS surveys—the Multiple Worksite Report and the Annual Refiling Survey.[7] To take another example, statistics on the national prison population use state correctional data sent to the Bureau of Justice Statistics (BJS) to provide descriptive statistics on the national correctional population. BJS is currently engaged in a significant effort to improve crime reporting by transitioning from the Uniform Crime Reports to the National Incident-Based Reporting System,[8] but this initiative requires cooperation and capacity from local criminal justice organizations. At the time of this writing, there has been insufficient support to develop the high-quality

---

[6]See: https://datasmart.ash.harvard.edu

[7]See: https://www.bls.gov/respondents/mwr/ and https://www.bls.gov/respondents/ars/faqs.htm

[8]For more information, see: https://www.fbi.gov/services/cjis/ucr/nibrs

data product that BJS envisioned. State resource and data-sharing challenges have significantly limited the impact of this important program (Moyer, 2021).

However, many valuable state, tribal, local, and territory government data are not accessible for statistical purposes. Like federal administrative data assets, many state-collected and state-maintained high-value administrative data assets, including those associated with federally funded programs, have statutory restrictions on access and use and are not funded to adequately curate their data. For example, unemployment insurance wages and claims records are not available to BLS (ILR School, 2021).

Similarly, BLS and the U.S. Census Bureau are prohibited from accessing the National Directory of New Hires, which contains person-level wage records compiled from all 50 states and the District of Columbia.[9] Even though federal statistical agencies routinely request administrative data from states and localities, states and localities are under no legal obligation to provide those data—even if the states' data collections are federally funded—given the federalized design of governments. There is no default that state-collected data from programs funded by the federal government must be shared back with federal agencies. Statutory changes are necessary to achieve this outcome. The Commission on Evidence-Based Policymaking's report, *The Promise of Evidence-Based Policymaking: Report of the Commission on Evidence-Based Policymaking*, recognized the value of blending data from state administrative agencies to create blended statistical products: "The Congress and the President should enact statutory or other changes to ensure state-collected administrative data on quarterly earnings...be available for statistical purposes and through a single federal source" (Commission on Evidence-Based Policymaking, 2017, Recommendation 2-6, pp. 44–45). Further, "The President should direct Federal departments that acquire state-collected administrative to make them available for statistical purposes" (Commission on Evidence-Based Policymaking, 2017, Recommendation 2-7, p. 45).

For the following discussions of a new data infrastructure, the panel assumes that these CEP recommendations will be realized (see Chapter 5). This report outlines a more comprehensive vision of a new data infrastructure built upon the foundation of CEP's proposals. The panel concludes, like CEP, the Markle Foundation, and earlier National Academies' Committee on National Statistics reports, that a new data infrastructure should include state, tribal, territory, and local government data assets, creating blended statistics of greater value.

---

[9]The directory is compiled by the Office of Child Support Enforcement in the U.S. Department of Health and Human Services. The data are used for enforcement purposes, as well as for specific program integrity, implementation, and research programs.

Private Sector Enterprises

Over the past few years, the growth of digital private sector data has vastly overwhelmed the growth of federal statistical agency data. In its December 2021 workshops on The Scope, Components, and Key Characteristics of a 21st Century Data Infrastructure, the panel considered opportunities, lessons learned, and challenges associated with using private sector data and blending private data with survey and administrative data. In an earlier report, the National Academies recommended that "Federal statistical agencies should systematically review their statistical portfolios and evaluate the potential benefits of using private sector data source" (the National Academies, 2017a, p. 64). Similarly, the Markle Foundation report (see Chapter 2) recommends leveraging new data, including private sector data (Markle Foundation, 2021).

As discussed in Chapter 2, 12 out of the 13 designated federal statistical agencies are using private sector data, and these uses can be expected to increase; for example, BEA reported the use of 142 different private sector data assets (Reamer, 2021). BEA's Health Satellite Account blends survey data from the Medical Expenditure Panel Survey with data from a private insurance company and Medicare claims data (Bohman, 2021). As another example, the U.S. National Survey of Early Care and Education conducted by the Administration on Children and Families measures the availability and use of childcare facilities. Real estate and property tax data from Zillow were used to enhance the quality of this traditional sample survey of households and providers (Datta et al., 2020).

As the panel learned in its December 2021 workshops, outside the United States, similar work is occurring at Statistics Netherlands, the U.K. Office of National Statistics, and Statistics Canada. Statistics Canada is requesting weekly store-level point-of-sale data from selected retail industries, to improve consumer price indexes (Statistics Canada, 2021). These initiatives both improve economic statistics and provide the basis for statistics of value to private firms. In other cases, Statistics Canada, like U.S. statistical agencies, pays private companies for access to data. Statistics Netherlands' Statistics Act includes broad powers requiring companies to share data with the Central Bureau of Statistics.[10]

At its 2022 conference, the American Economic Association Committee on Statistics (AEAStat) recognized the potential benefits of using high-frequency private sector data to "modernize official statistics."[11] AEAStat

---

[10]For more information on Netherlands' Central Bureau of Statistics, see: https://www.cbs.nl/en-gb/about-us/organisation

[11]A video of the session can be found here: https://www.aeaweb.org/conference/2022/aea-session-recordings/player?meetingId=732&recordingId=1236&VideoSearch%5Bpage%5D=0

proposes that statistical agencies "connect" to data behind companies' firewalls using software that accesses the companies' data lakes and provides aggregated statistics, not microdata, to the statistical agency or a third-party data repository. AEAStat has proposed a demonstration project involving 5–10 large retailers, to test the idea's feasibility.

On February 21st, 2022, the European Commission published a call for evidence, related to the *European Statistical System—making it fit for the future*.[12] The document requests feedback regarding the proposal to make new data sources available for official statistics and statistical purposes. The proposal would extend the provisions of the recently proposed Data Act (European Commission, 2022). Among the provisions of the Data Act, if eventually enacted, is to require compulsory business-to-government data sharing for official statistics.

For all the promise of commercial data, private sector data are not without limitations. Like administrative data, private sector data are collected for a purpose different from that of data for use in a national data infrastructure. Business interests often preclude companies from capturing data about everyone, which introduces notable biases and equity challenges in the data. The data items companies capture do not always enable easy linkage or use the same standards common among federal data users or they may lack adequate documentation or metadata, all complicating replicability. Moreover, multinational corporations must abide by the laws of each involved nation, many of which prevent the provision of residents' or citizens' data to foreign governments without explicit consent. Another challenge of relying on data from private firms is that changes in firm strategy, management, or ownership can disrupt data sharing, either because of changes to the collected data or changes in the willingness of firms to share data. In the panel's view, these technical, jurisdictional, organizational, and equity challenges must be evaluated and considered before acquiring private sector data assets. Chapter 2 described the limitations of private sector data highlighted during the panel's December workshops. Still, private sector data can fill gaps in other data sources, and they remain an untapped asset.

As mentioned earlier, CEP and the Evidence Act are silent regarding accessing and using private sector data. Benefits from a blended approach would include a more comprehensive understanding of important national conditions, smoother trends, more reasonable estimates, and more data granularity. The panel concluded, as did the earlier evaluations mentioned above, that private sector data assets offer opportunities to improve national statistics and support more rigorous social and economic research.

---

[12]See: https://ec.europa.eu/info/law/better-regulation/have-your-say/initiatives/13332-European-Statistical-System-making-it-fit-for-the-future_en

Data Brokers

Data brokers collect, buy, aggregate, and sell data on individuals and companies for profit. Data brokers collect information from a wide variety of public records, including arrest records, marriage licenses, property records, building permits, and digital sources like cookies, browser fingerprinting, web beacons, and IP address tracking (Melendez and Pasternack, 2019). Data brokers also purchase and resell customer data from other companies, notably during bankruptcy auctions.

Combined information is sold for a variety of purposes, including verifying identity, marketing products and services, building consumer profiles, and detecting fraud. Data brokers sell information to a variety of customers. Some data brokers, like CoreLogic, blend diverse data sources to develop innovative products. CoreLogic blends collected data from 5.5 billion property records—more than a billion visual records including aerial photos, home tours, and interactive floor plans—and several hundred analytical models that extrapolate raw data into an entire portfolio of products that CoreLogic sells to companies and government agencies, including statistical agencies.[13] Experian, Transunion, and Equifax assemble data from consumers' credit-related actions and provide reports to individuals, as well as to other businesses for advertising and marketing purposes (Irby, 2022).

Data brokers, however, rarely interact directly with consumers. Consumers generally do not provide their express permission or consent for data brokers to use their data, and consumers are often unaware of the existence or practices of such brokers. Data-broker data are notoriously rife with errors that consumers cannot correct. Data brokers are almost entirely unregulated, with no federal laws regulating businesses that buy and sell personal information. Only two states, Vermont and California, have enacted data-broker laws (Wilkie et al., n.d.).

While data brokers are private sector entities, they are discussed separately in this report because their business model and incentives for sharing data set them apart. The use of data brokers also introduces more complicated consent and ethics issues, quality challenges, and the possibility of future state and federal regulations.

Data from brokers rarely link easily with agency data, and these vendors frequently overpromise their products (Studds, 2021). One advantage of data from brokers is that brokers will have already aligned the data models from diverse public and private sources to accomplish their business purposes; however, the transformations required for alignment with statistical agencies' data may degrade data quality and not reflect the

---

[13]For more information, see: https://www.corelogic.com/why-corelogic/

priorities of those agencies. This can raise important issues of data equity, as people with few financial resources may disappear or be aggregated in misleading ways that make sense for an individual data user but that would be fundamentally at odds with the goals of a statistical agency. Requesting sample or proof-of-concept data from data brokers can help to overcome some risks, as can requesting raw data rather than derived data products. Importantly, Studds (2021) emphasized the importance of statistical agencies maintaining good relationships with third-party data holders, to fulfill the legal obligations of the statistical agency.

Data-broker data assets and the many issues they raise warrant careful evaluation before inclusion in a new data infrastructure.

Nonprofit and Academic Institutions

The data resources produced and made available by U.S. universities and research institutions are key components of the current national data infrastructure. Academic institutions create and provide access to valuable data assets, such as the Panel Study of Income Dynamics,[14] the General Social Survey,[15] the Health and Retirement Study,[16] the National Longitudinal Study of Adolescent to Adult Health,[17] the Survey of Consumers,[18] and the American National Election Studies.[19] Some other nonprofit research groups, like the Pew Research Center, also conduct surveys that are placed in the public domain. Many of these surveys are national in scope and provide important aggregate indicators of key characteristics of the population. Each survey also provides microdata to the statistical and research communities, either directly or through the Inter-university Consortium for Political and Social Research (ICPSR)[20] or the Roper Center.

Many of these university-based studies have been innovators in the use of blended data, through activities including linking to administrative data; collecting and integrating biological, streaming, audio, visual, and video data; and working with private data holders. In several cases, collaborations between university-based studies and statistical agencies have facilitated the creation of more detailed and timely data covering subjects not well served by the existing infrastructure of statistical agencies.

---

[14] See: https://psidonline.isr.umich.edu/

[15] See: https://gss.norc.org/

[16] See: https://hrs.isr.umich.edu/welcome-health-and-retirement-study

[17] See: https://addhealth.cpc.unc.edu/

[18] See: https://data.sca.isr.umich.edu/

[19] See: https://electionstudies.org/about-us/

[20] ICPSR disseminates the Family Self-Sufficiency Program, AdHealth, Survey of Consumers, and Monitoring the Future data, in some cases in addition to dissemination by the data producer. See: https://www.icpsr.umich.edu/

Some nonprofit organizations provide direct public access to their data, including the leadership and financial features of their organizations, as in Guidestar.org.[21] The current national statistical infrastructure benefits from these collaborations, which can sometimes make use of the greater flexibility outside the federal government, tap into academic talent, and access alternate sources of funding.

The promise of these data could be enhanced through increased sharing with federal and state statistical and administrative resources when permitted. Both their value as research vehicles and their worth as national informational resources could be improved by blending them with the nation's other data resources. Ongoing and strengthened collaborations with academic organizations also provide an important source of continued innovation (Jarmin, 2019).

Crowdsourced or Citizen-Science Data Holders

The use of crowdsourced data or volunteered data purposefully collected and assembled by the public to support information assets has emerged as an increasingly significant source of data that can also be used to guide official decisionmaking. Powerful data-collection devices like cell phones, sensors, and other components of the "internet of things" are nearly ubiquitous in the modern landscape, enabling individuals, businesses, governments, and civil society to collaborate around data sourcing—from the crowd. Similarly, the increasing occurrence of citizen-science projects like the COVID Tracking Project[22] across a range of social, economic, and environmental applications, offer not only new data sources but also data interpretation, validation, corroboration, and other actions that provide a rich new source for blending data. Coupled with new communications technologies and social media, these advances now reach even more people through internet connectivity, and open platforms exist not only for using data but also for creating it. Crowdsourced geospatial data are one prominent example, given the GPS features of cell phones. Public participation in spatial data creation through open mapping, such as the U.S. Geological Survey's The National Map,[23] has empowered citizens to provide knowledge and context to open-map resources (Goodchild, 2007). Crowdsourced data offer the opportunity to "collectively produce finer-grained and more expansive data sets over regional and global scales and collect data more frequently, covering long temporal extents" compared to alternative methods (Fischer et al., 2021, p. 2).

---

[21] See: GuideStar nonprofit reports and Forms 990 for donors, grantmakers, and businesses: https://www.guidestar.org/

[22] See: https://covidtracking.com/

[23] See: https://www.usgs.gov/programs/national-geospatial-program/national-map

Statistical inquiries about blending crowdsourced data with other data are now ongoing. For example, Buil-Gil et al. (2020) review the use of small-area estimation techniques to improve crowdsourced data about public safety in London. Much of these crowdsourced data do not rely on standard statistical geographic designations, such as counties. Blending geospatial data with statistical survey data and other data sources is complex[24] and warrants additional attention and research.

While these technological advances have grown the amount of available data immensely, concerns about crowdsourced data and information derived from citizen science parallel the limitations of commercial data. As with private sector data, nonstandard collection realities mean that the blending of crowdsourced data into official government databases systematically suffers from a lack of trust in data quality, uncertainty about adherence to standards, and frequent incompleteness. Crowdsourced data are not always produced with an awareness of the demands required to successfully implement evidence-based decisionmaking in government agencies. However, in the panel's opinion, public engagement through purposeful crowdsourcing could represent an opportunity for greater awareness and appreciation of a new data infrastructure or the use of data as evidence. Moreover, since many citizen science and crowdsourcing initiatives stem from a desire to support the public interest, working with these communities to co-construct standards and measure limitations may be especially productive. The COVID Tracking Project is a good example of how volunteers could identify limitations and data lags in state-reported data and provide states with timely, useful feedback.

Box 4-2 lists the data holders whose data should be available for possible inclusion in a new data infrastructure.

The Evidence Act, once fully enacted, will make the federal statistical agency and federal program and administrative data assets available to the data infrastructure, when not prohibited by law. Nonprofit tax data are already available. The IRS requires all U.S. tax-exempt nonprofits to make public their three most recent annual IRS Form 990s; access to academic institutions' data assets of interest to the data infrastructure will occur contractually. Crowdsourced data assets are also publicly available and accessible. However, in the panel's judgment, a new data infrastructure will not realize the promise of improved blended statistics until the data assets held by the state, tribal, territory, and local governments and the private sector are included.

---

[24]See: United Nations Guide to Data Integration for Official Statistics: https://statswiki. unece.org/display/DI/Guide+to+Data+Integration+for+Official+Statistics

---

BOX 4-2
Data Holders Proposed to Share Data in a
21st Century National Data Infrastructure

- Principal federal statistical agencies
- Federal program and administrative agencies
- State, tribal, territory, and local governments
- Private sector enterpriseås
- Data brokers
- Nonprofit and academic institutions
- Crowdsourced or citizen science

SOURCE: Panel generated.

Data from federal, state, tribal, territory, and local governments; the private sector; nonprofits and academic institutions; and crowdsourced and citizen-science data holders are crucial components of a 21st century national data infrastructure. (Conclusion 4-1)

In the panel's ideal vision, easily accessible, comprehensive catalogs of data assets would be a key feature of a new data infrastructure. Catalogs would be easily searchable so that the public, data subjects, data holders, data users, researchers, and key stakeholders would be informed of the extent of the infrastructure. The searchable catalogs or inventories would contain metadata describing the contents of the data assets, the provenance of the data, any known limitations to the data, and which data subjects are implicated. While some progress has been made, in the panel's opinion much more needs to be done to make data assets discoverable, accessible, and usable.

Some data inventories or catalogs of diverse data holdings do exist at the federal level. The National Archives and Records Administration (NARA), in its role as the official archive for many federal statistics, has developed the National Archives Catalog for users to search and access its collection. The catalog "searches across multiple National Archives resources at once, including archival descriptions, digitized and electronic records, authority records, and web pages from Archives.gov and the Presidential Libraries" (National Archives, 2021). Without such a catalog and related query system, accessing NARA records could not be done efficiently. However, the catalog includes only those records formally sent to NARA by federal agencies and is, thus, incomplete. Similarly, ICPSR maintains an online, searchable catalog of justice-related data.[25] In addition, most federal statistical agencies maintain online documentation of their data assets. Many of the restricted data assets of the federal statistical system are now described with standardized metadata in a single application portal.[26]

Sometime soon, there will be a comprehensive inventory of federal-government data assets. The Evidence Act (U.S. Congress, 2019, Section 3511) requires every federal agency to develop and maintain comprehensive data inventories of all their data assets. The inventory will include the name, the metadata (including all variable names and definitions), the data owner, any restrictions on the use of the data asset, and criteria used in determining why a data asset is not publicly available. The Federal Chief Data Officer (CDO) Council established a Data Inventory Working Group in March 2021 "to improve the efficiency and effectiveness of federal data inventories" (Federal CDO Council, n.d., "Goals"). The Evidence Act also requires the administrator of general services to maintain a single public online interface, called the Federal Data Catalogue. At the time of this writing, some of these Evidence Act mandates have not yet been implemented.

Currently there is also no central inventory of nonfederal-government data assets. In the panel's opinion, the absence of such a catalog will hamper data discovery and forego opportunities for expanded data access and use.

WHICH DATA SHOULD BE INCLUDED?

Not all existing data, even if accessible, will serve the country's important information needs. Some data contain information crucial to the future understanding of the welfare of society (e.g., health, employment); others may be less important (e.g., length of major league baseball games). Which of the key data-holding groups should be part of a new data infrastructure, and which of their held data should be prioritized in a new infrastructure? In this section, a set of criteria is proffered that the panel considers potentially useful for choosing which data to include in a new data infrastructure.

Fitness-for-Use to Produce Key Information for the Country

The priority might be data assets measuring social and economic attributes of widespread research and policymaking relevance. Some of these data are already collected but very imperfectly (e.g., prices and quantities of retail goods sold). Some of these data have been studied in one-time research projects but have never been systematically reported on a national basis (e.g., alternative measures of the gig economy, Abraham et al., 2021).

---

[25] See: https://www.icpsr.umich.edu/web/pages/ICPSR/index.html
[26] See: www.ResearchDataGov.org

Others reveal gaps between commercial and public-sector frames (e.g., real estate development data[27] versus census geography frames).

Data assets should be uniquely suited and fit for the intended use. That is, in contrast to assembling all data of *potential* interest, pre-specified important questions of critical importance must precede data access. Data useful to answer those questions should be given priority, in the panel's opinion. Accessible tools, aligned incentives, and broad applicability of data provide conditions for data fit for use (Bohman, 2021). Necessity demands that the data asset generates statistical information and tangible benefits to the public, data users, and data holders.

Determining the fitness-for-use of a given data source requires clear articulation of quality standards for specific uses. In 2017, the Federal Committee on Statistical Methodology (FCSM) established a Working Group on Transparent Quality Reporting in the Integration of Multiple Data Sources, to identify best practices associated with data-quality measurement and reporting for blended data products. This work was motivated by the increasing use of alternative and blended data by statistical agencies and by the Committee on National Statistics' Panel on Improving Federal Statistics for Policy and Social Science Research Using Multiple Data Sources and State-of-the Art Estimation, described in Chapter 2.

A National Academies' report reviewed the long-established quality frameworks for survey data (as in Groves and Lyberg, 2010) and recommended statistical agencies adopt a broader data-quality framework while concluding that "Commonly used existing metrics for reporting survey quality may fall short in providing sufficient information for evaluating survey quality" (the National Academies, 2017b, p. 114). The report also pointed out the importance of focusing more attention on the tradeoffs among various quality dimensions, such as trading precision for timeliness and granularity rather than focusing primarily on accuracy.

The FCSM Working Group, along with the Washington Statistical Society, responded to this suggestion by sponsoring several public workshops (Brown et al., 2018). The workshops were complemented by a report by Mathematica Policy Research, sponsored by the Statistics of Income Division at the Internal Revenue Service, that examined international quality frameworks. Mathematica found that countries nearly uniformly defined quality as fitness-for-use (Czajka and Stange, 2018). Also, internationally, data quality in each of the various quality frameworks is considered multidimensional (i.e., not just reflecting the quality of measurements but also the quality of representativeness of the population of interest).

The FCSM Working Group published *A Framework for Data Quality* in September 2020. The report provided a framework for identifying data

---

[27]See: https://cherre.com/

quality for all data, recognizing the opportunities and challenges of new data sources, and noting the growing reliance on integrating data from multiple sources. The report defines quality as "the degree to which data captures the desired information using appropriate methodology in a manner that sustains public trust" (Federal Committee on Statistical Methodology, 2020, p. 6). The definition applies to all data, data products, and analytical products. It also applies to the entire data file as well as individual data elements. It applies to traditional methods as well as new and emerging methods such as artificial intelligence and machine learning. The definition also applies to diverse data sources as well as integrated data, also often referred to as blended, combined, or linked data.

The framework uses three broad domains and 11 data-quality dimensions as shown in Table 4-1.

This framework documents threats to data quality associated with each of the dimensions included in the framework. Identifying these threats is a necessary first step in "mitigation, managing trade-offs among them, and for reporting data quality" (Federal Committee on Statistical Methodology, 2020, p. 5). The report includes best practices to identify data-quality threats.

Data Minimized to Satisfy Pre-Specified Purposes

In the panel's view, a new data infrastructure should not result in the unbridled harvesting of all digital data that exists in the country. Instead, the data-acquisition request—the records, data elements, data granularity, and frequency—should be limited to the information needed to satisfy the proposed statistical purpose. Statistics Canada has used such a framework for the intake of data according to necessity and proportionality criteria, where proportionality means that Statistics Canada takes no more than is needed and considers the sensitivity and confidentiality of the data (Bowlby, 2021).

A similar approach could prove prudent for the United States, in the panel's opinion. A disciplined approach to a new data infrastructure implies that the information needs of the country (necessity) determine which data items are included. Besides focusing on minimizing the volume of data records and associated data elements acquired, the minimization principle implies a judgment regarding the level of detail and the frequency of access needed to satisfy the statistical purpose(s). A statistical purpose requiring the linking of statistical-agency data assets with data holders' microdata will be more consequential than a statistical purpose that can be satisfied with aggregated data, such as the production of monthly retail sales. That said, conditions and needs can change over time. As such, flexible contracts that include multiple-year options and the potential for expanded coverage might prove logistically prudent during negotiations with private sector data holders (Bohman, 2021).

TABLE 4-1 Dimensions of Data Quality

Domain	Dimension	Definition
UTILITY	Relevance	Relevance refers to whether the data product is targeted to meet current and prospective user needs.
	Accessibility	Accessibility relates to the ease with which data users can obtain an agency's products and documentation in forms and formats that are understandable to data users.
	Timeliness	Timeliness is the length of time between the event or phenomenon the data describe and their availability.
	Punctuality	Punctuality is measured as the time lag between the actual release of the data and the planned target date for data release.
	Granularity	Granularity refers to the amount of disaggregation available for key data elements. Granularity can be expressed in units of time, level of geographic detail available, or the amount of detail available on any of many characteristics (e.g., demographic, socio-economic).
OBJECTIVITY	Accuracy and Reliability	Accuracy measures the closeness of an estimate from a data product to its true value. Reliability, a related concept, characterizes the consistency of results when the same phenomenon is measured or estimated more than once under similar conditions.
	Coherence	Coherence is the ability of the data products to maintain common definitions, classifications, and methodological processes, to align with external statistical standards, and to maintain consistency and comparability with other relevant data.
INTEGRITY	Scientific Integrity	Scientific integrity refers to an environment that ensures adherence to scientific standards and use of established scientific methods to produce and disseminate objective data products and one that shields these products from inappropriate political influence.
	Credibility	Credibility characterizes the confidence that users place in data products based simply on the qualifications and past performance of the data producer.
	Computer and physical security	Computer and physical security of data refers to the protection of information throughout the collection, production, analysis, and development process from unauthorized access or revision to ensure that the information is not compromised through corruption or falsification.
	Confidentiality	Confidentiality refers to a quality or condition of information as an obligation not to disclose that information to an unauthorized party.

SOURCE: Federal Committee on Statistical Methodology, 2020, Table ES1, p. 4.

Data Access and Use Respect Data Holders' and
Data Subjects' Interests and Privacy

In the panel's vision, a new data infrastructure's requests to acquire, access, and use data assets for statistical purposes must respect the reputation and interests of data holders and data subjects. Private companies, for example, have minimal incentives to share data with statistical agencies, and often think the perceived risks (e.g., high costs, intrusive practices, reputation risks) outweigh any possible benefits (e.g., money or personalized statistics).

Creating devices like schemas, application program interfaces (APIs), and legal arrangements can help reduce friction and risks to data owners, as Matthew Shapiro, a workshop participant, noted. In the panel's view, leveraging state-of-the-art privacy and security tools is essential. Respecting data-holder interests and the privacy of data subjects can be further supported by carefully considering the level of detail needed, the frequency requested, and the way data are acquired and potentially linked. In the panel's vision of a new data infrastructure, procedures should be in place to ensure data use is responsible, ethical, and equitable. This may include working with data holders to effectively communicate with data subjects and evaluate consent-related issues. Alternatively, this may involve ensuring that the data received from data holders cannot be re-identified. A new data infrastructure should actively engage data holders to develop a range of possible approaches that could help ensure responsible data exchange.

Prioritize Easily Acquired Data That Provide Tangible Benefits

While the most important criteria for inclusion of data in a new data infrastructure involve utility to the country's informational needs, some data access may require unusually complicated logistical challenges. Thus, in the panel's judgment, the costs and efforts incurred by both the data holder and the statistical agency (or acquiring entity) should be proportionate to the anticipated public benefits associated with the proposed statistical purpose. Statistical agencies should have procedures in place to quantify data-holder and statistical-agency costs as well as anticipated public benefits. The use of passively collected data, for example, can reduce the burden on data holders and provide more timely statistics, particularly in the healthcare sector (Moyer, 2021). In the panel's view, data assets should be acquired and used only if the associated costs and effort are not disproportionate to their benefits.

Access to data requires an investment of time and resources. Easily accessed data should be given priority, but using trial or sample data can help to identify potential challenges and expedite the evaluation of benefit

(Stevens, 2021). Private data, according to Sarah Henry, a workshop participant, are not like "gold dust" but rather like sand, abundant and requiring significant effort to make them useful. Early evaluations should consider potential choke points in data collection, the sustainability of data, the representativeness of the data, and ways to correct for bias.

Available, Usable Metadata Is Essential for Statistical Purposes

Aggregation over records containing variable entries is meaningless unless one knows what each variable means. In surveys and censuses, the meaning of entries is specified before data collection. This becomes the basis of information about the data, the "metadata" of the dataset. If a data holder uses data for a single purpose, metadata may not be as valued as in research and statistical organizations. To be used for approved statistical purposes, these data must be described by metadata. For potentially valuable data assets lacking usable metadata, the metadata need to be developed and available to possible data users. A data infrastructure entity may collaborate with the data holder to develop the necessary documentation.

In the panel's judgment, metadata are critical for blended data uses. To be responsibly discovered, combined, shared, used, and reused, data must be described. Limitations of data must also be readily accessible to ensure that biases in individual data assets do not ripple through any analysis. Metadata, using standard reusable schemas, permit the automation of data analysis, data transfer, and aggregation. In the panel's vision, a new data infrastructure requires a comprehensive metadata repository with a user interface to facilitate and automate data discovery, sharing, use, processing, and protection. As noted by Ivan Deloach, workshop participant, metadata may be helpful when addressing the benefits and costs related to data quality and representativeness.

While statistical agencies have attempted to establish metadata standards within their organizations, there is no single standard for the federal statistical system. A recently released report from the National Academies identifies three categories of metadata: descriptive (facilitates discovery and identification), structural (describes how compound objects are put together), and administrative (information to help manage a resource) (the National Academies, 2022). The machine-learning community has proposed using the concept of datasheets for datasets as an approach for standardizing metadata (Gebru et al., 2021).

The panel does not take a stand on the desirability of a unique metadata standard. Instead, it envisions an infrastructure that can adapt to a variety of metadata structures, as well as evolve over time. In the panel's vision, the minimal threshold of acceptability of a metadata approach is that it informs the blending of data from multiple sources with sufficient

---

BOX 4-3
Key Characteristics of Data Assets to Be Included
in a 21st Century National Data Infrastructure

- Assets are fit for intended statistical purposes.
- Acquisition of information is limited and minimized to satisfy pre-specified purpose.
- Access and use respect data holders' and data subjects' interests and privacy.
- Uses should prioritize easily acquired data assets that provide tangible benefits.
- Available, usable metadata to facilitate statistical uses.

SOURCE: Panel generated.

---

understanding of the meaning of data items and the limitations of each data asset.

Box 4-3 summarizes the criteria of data that, according to the panel's vision, should be included in a 21st century national data infrastructure.

BLENDED DATA REQUIRE NEW STATISTICAL METHODS

There is much to learn from past and future efforts regarding the blending of multiple data sources to improve the quality of statistical information. Organizations are now discovering when blending diverse data assets can improve existing statistics, satisfy emerging or unmet data needs, decrease reporting burden, and address issues of quality, bias, and data equity. Combining diverse data sources also provides the opportunity to produce timelier, more granular, and higher-frequency statistics, as needed. For example, Antonio Chessa, a workshop participant, noted that using transaction data in the Consumer Price Index—which focuses on business-consumer transactions and increased granularity in time and item—can improve price-index methods and statistics with greater temporal and spatial detail.

Yet, in pursuit of these benefits, statistical agencies and researchers face increasing challenges as they move from using a single data source to incorporating secondary sources, such as administrative datasets—the challenges increase when attempting to incorporate additional data assets from the private sector, state, tribal, and local governments, or crowdsourced or citizen-science sources. Whenever two or more different data sources are combined, the challenges increase. Workshop presenters noted that private-sector data rarely come in the desired form even though they are often useful. Some presenters recommended that a whole set of new methods, including statistical design, would be needed to ingest and integrate blended data assets on a large scale.

Fortunately, much work has already been done, both identifying the challenges of combining multiple data sources and suggesting approaches for combining them appropriately. A National Academies' report (the National Academies, 2017b) summarized statistical methods that can be used for combining data from multiple sources, highlighting the following:

- Record linkage: The report provides an extensive discussion of record linkage, providing numerous examples of agencies and programs that are using record linkage for research and for producing statistics.[28] The examples illustrate the benefits of record linkage, but the report points out that record linkage is not a panacea. Linkage rates vary across studies and for subpopulations within studies. Record linkage usually requires that data for individual entities be available from the data sources, along with sufficient identifying information to allow records to be linked. If these criteria are not met, other methods are needed.

- Multiple frame methods: A multiple-frame survey draws samples from two or more sampling frames, to improve coverage of the population or to decrease costs. Typically, multiple-frame surveys are associated with less privacy intrusion than record linkage, but it is important to understand possible differences in data-collection methods and the completeness of each frame. Alternative data sources could be used to construct supplemental frames at a lower cost, albeit at some loss in coverage.

- Imputation-based methods: Another way to conceptualize combining different data sources may be by using a missing data framework and imputing the missing data based on statistical models. The report discusses statistical matching methods and software for this purpose, but staff expertise and continuous training are needed, particularly in evolving technologies common to modern computer science, including database, cryptography, privacy-preserving, and privacy-enhancing technologies (the National Academies, 2017b). The opportunities and challenges are discussed in detail.

- Modeling techniques: In cases in which record linkage, imputation, or the multiple-frames approach are inappropriate, another statistical modeling can be used to combine aggregated statistics or with individual-records data when the data sources measure different variables (the National Academies, 2017b). The report discusses

---

[28] An important consideration for a new data infrastructure is the attitudes of data subjects regarding linkage of their data, as presented in Fobia et al. (2020).

small-area estimation methods but suggests that combining new models needs empirical testing and substantive justification.

The report recommends the following steps for the federal statistical system:

- Systematically coordinate federal agencies' efforts to blend multiple data sources;
- Ensure that statistical agencies have the appropriate skills and expertise (the National Academies, 2017b); and
- Encourage federal agencies to develop partnerships with academia and encourage external research organizations to develop methods needed for design and analysis using multiple data sources.

BLENDED DATA REQUIRE NEW STATISTICAL DESIGNS

As a new data infrastructure evolves, in the panel's view no single data-sourcing strategy will be optimal for all informational needs. Each data source (e.g., surveys, administrative records, or private sector data) has some weakness regarding the population coverage, relevance of measurement, timeliness, and granularity of potential statistical aggregates. Past reviews (e.g., the National Academies, 2017a,b) have speculated that, after initial blended data estimates are available, a new period of statistical design might usefully take place, to find approaches that make use of the strengths of multiple sources.

For example, data on the access and delivery of health services exist from government agencies (e.g., Medicare and Medicaid) but also from household health surveys, hospital samples, electronic record platforms, and a variety of other sources. In the panel's opinion, after new blended statistics using multiple data sources are built, that survey designs could likely be optimized, reducing original survey measurement in populations that are well measured and increasing survey measurement in populations not well covered by the various administrative record systems. In some cases, this may yield a reduction in statistical agency budgets allocated to original data collections and an increase in budgets devoted to accessing shared records.

BLENDED DATA REQUIRE NEW DATA INFRASTRUCTURE CAPABILITIES

In the 20th century, the data ecosystem of businesses and administrative government agencies rested on entities independently designing data for their particular uses. Since the data were used principally by those who designed them, data required little documentation and no preparation for access by others. Since most data were used for a specific purpose at a specific point in time, consistency over time was subordinate to utility for the specified use. Any data manipulation or transformation was singularly focused on immediate organizational needs. If multiple data sources were needed, integrating software would be "hard-coded" into the design.

Government statistical agencies designed their data programs to monitor important social and economic conditions for populations of interest. The statistical data were held closely and securely by those agencies, as part of their confidentiality pledges to data holders and subjects. The statistics produced from the data were released according to preset schedules, rarely more often than monthly.

In the panel's vision, such data silos no longer serve the needs of modern society. Features of the 20th century data infrastructure must change to achieve the panel's vision for a new data infrastructure. As an increasing number of initiatives occur, combining data from multiple independent sources, further desirable capabilities of a new data infrastructure are articulated. Box 4-4 lists work by the United Nations' Economic Commission on Europe's High-Level Data Group for Modernization of Statistical Production and Services related to a Common Statistical Data Architecture (CSDA), an initiative aimed at consistently describing the data aspects of statistical production.[29] The group identified high-level capabilities required by a new data infrastructure to realize the promise of blending multiple data sources. Capabilities require the interaction of organizations, people, processes, and technology and generally describe the "what and why" of statistical production, not the "how and who."

A new data infrastructure will require enhanced capabilities. While there is much existent talent for documenting data designed for statistical uses (e.g., surveys and censuses), there is less expertise available for documenting those features of administrative and process data that were never intended to be used in statistical operations. Similarly, Box 4-4 notes the need to define and track supply chains of data, to access data in diverse locations simultaneously, and to work with a set of partners deserving ongoing support. Data integration is well exercised in some organizations, but not all, especially for datasets that were not originally designed to be used in tandem. While data governance is well documented in federal statistical agencies, it was originally designed for data assets that would be fully acquired and stored behind the agencies' firewalls, not for a world in which data assets are too large to move from organization to organization. Finally, knowledge management—the ability to understand differences among measures found in multiple datasets—is critical for the statistical operations needed to blend data into more informative estimates.

---

[29]See: https://statswiki.unece.org/display/DA/CSDA+2.0

BOX 4-4
Capabilities Needed for a 21st Century
National Data Infrastructure

- Requiring Enhancement Over Current Practices
- *Data design, definition, and description of data not originally built for statistical analysis
- *Data logistics, managing supply chains between data holders and data users
- *Data sharing support, accessing data from and returning statistical information to partners
- Data transformation, the ability to transform data to make them suitable for specific uses and purposes
- *Data integration, the ability to combine, link, relate, and/or align data assets from multiple sources
- *Data governance, the ability to manage data assets by defining and enforcing established policies, processes, and rules in accordance with strategic objectives
- Security and data assurance, protecting and maintaining data assets, at rest and in-transit
- Provenance and lineage, tracking the edition and source of a given version of a data asset
- *Knowledge management, documenting the meaning of individual measurements on data assets

---

NOTE: *Capabilities the panel views as novel to some of the partners/stakeholders participating in a new data infrastructure.

SOURCE: Adapted from United Nations Economic Commission for Europe on behalf of the international statistical community: https://statswiki.unece.org/display/DA/CSDA+2.0. Reproduced under Creative Commons Attribution 3.0 International License (https://creativecommons.org/licenses/by/3.0/).

In the panel's estimation, these skills can be acquired by the organizations involved in a new infrastructure, but only with intentionality. For example, full engagement of the academic sector can provide critical capacities like analytical expertise, upskilling existing organizational skills, and educating the future workforce, so that agencies can operate nimbly and dynamically in a new data infrastructure.

BLENDED DATA POSE NEW PRIVACY
AND ETHICAL CHALLENGES

A 21st century national data infrastructure cannot succeed without ensuring ethical exchange of data; trust in institutions involved in data exchange; privacy-preserving techniques; and technical, organizational, and legal mechanisms supporting responsible data practices. For the latter half of the 20th century, these concerns were collectively categorized as "privacy." Privacy has multiple definitions in legal and technical contexts, but colloquially the concept of "privacy" is employed when people are concerned that they lack meaningful control over a social situation and the information flowing in that context (Marwick and boyd, 2014). In the 21st century, a wider range of concepts are deployed to define privacy. Data collections and use that respect privacy are thought of as ethical, trustworthy, and responsible.

In the panel's view, ethical treatment of data subjects requires adherence to four key values (see Chapter 3). First, the actions of a new infrastructure should be guided by attention to how use of a subject's data will affect that subject's life. Second, there are underlying issues of autonomy—the ability of individuals to make their own decisions. A new data infrastructure must recognize the nature of informed consent by the data subject. Third, there is a concern about beneficence—that is, to what extent will data be used to produce good outcomes for the data subject? Finally, there is a focus on human dignity—that is, are the activities of a new infrastructure conducted in a manner that is respectful of data subjects? Collectively, in the panel's opinion, these values must underlie both policy and practice. Only after these individual concerns are addressed can the societal benefits of improved statistical information be appreciated.

While these values must be fundamental to a data infrastructure, laws provide another framework for addressing the range of social, cultural, and reputational issues at play. In the 20th century, lawmakers passed numerous bills restricting government data collection and use. The laws that govern the private sector are more diverse. Moreover, while federal data holders must only concern themselves with federal laws, multinational corporations must grapple with privacy laws in numerous countries. Countries may have overlapping data regulations based on the data subject, location of the company's employees, and location of the company's data centers. While some companies may be required to share data (e.g., pollution levels from a manufacturer), others operate under voluntary agreements between users and data holders (e.g., credit-reporting data), and still others are legally prohibited from sharing certain kinds of data without explicit consent (e.g., healthcare, movie rentals). The legal procedures covering privacy are both complex and incomplete. Most importantly, the limitations of privacy laws infuriate data subjects, data holders, and data users for wholly distinct reasons.

Advances in computing have increased privacy-related risks while also enabling the development of privacy-enhancing technologies. Some new processes are specifically designed to support novel forms of statistical data sharing. For example, formal privacy protection provides a technical framework for balancing data accuracy and statistical confidentiality. The U.S. Census Bureau began releasing data using synthetic data generation in 2006, as part of its Longitudinal Employer-Household Dynamics program and has a formal privacy analysis of this data-anonymization process.[30] The National Institutes of Health (NIH), the National Institute for Standards and Technology, and the National Science Foundation (NSF) are all working to build standards around homomorphic encryption, to enable computation on encrypted data. Investments in developing privacy-enhancing technologies—including funding from NIH, NSF, and the Defense Advanced Research Projects Agency—and applying them to various data-user scenarios are ongoing. In the panel's judgment, tracking these technical mechanisms and integrating them into practice will increase data holders' confidence in sharing data.

Privacy laws and technologies can help strengthen data protections. As analysts in the federal statistical system aim to improve current deficiencies by integrating and blending multiple sources of data, they have come to realize that even when data are de-identified, linking sources increases risk of re-identification (Sweeney et al., 2017). Merely connecting the site of an individualized record to the same site of another can inadvertently reveal personally identifiable information that was obscured before blending. Methodologies to balance privacy tradeoffs, such as geomasking, can address the need to protect individuals while still enabling individual-level data to be utilized or analyzed without significantly affecting statistical results (Kwan et al., 2004).

However, prior attempts to centralize federal data assets have repeatedly been thwarted by pushback under the label of "privacy." The Privacy Act of 1974, for example, was created in direct response to a 1965 effort to create a National Data Center.[31] In response to this history, the Evidence Act put privacy front and center.

Meanwhile, however, the conversation has evolved. Federal government agencies and academia are speaking of trustworthy AI,[32] data ethics,[33] and data equity.[34] Practitioners in the industry use similar language, cognizant of how "trust" is dependent on being seen as "responsible." Data holders are engaged in robust conversations about "data governance," while representatives of data subjects are asking to be included in governing mechanisms.

---

[30]See: https://lehd.ces.census.gov/applications/help/onthemap.html#!what_is_onthemap

[31]For a discussion of the National Data Center and a thorough history of data-related privacy concerns see Igo (2018, Ch 6).

[32]See: https://www.ai.gov/strategic-pillars/advancing-trustworthy-ai/

[33]See: https://resources.data.gov/assets/documents/fds-data-ethics-framework.pdf

[34]See: https://covid19.census.gov/pages/data-equity

In the panel's judgment, a new data infrastructure must be attentive to—and in conversation with—the range of stakeholders engaging on these topics. While useful, privacy laws and technologies alone will not serve as an effective response to threats that could challenge the legitimacy of a new data infrastructure. Rather, all who are involved—including data subjects, data holders, and data users—must collectively negotiate best practices, governance mechanisms, and normative expectations about data exchange. This requires creating and sustaining a governing body (or set of bodies) tasked with building processes and practices, sustaining relationships with stakeholders, and ensuring that trade-offs are collectively negotiated.

MULTIPLE ORGANIZATIONAL STRUCTURES CAN SUPPORT A NEW DATA INFRASTRUCTURE

In this section, the panel does not suggest a specific organizational model but instead identifies assumptions regarding the data assets, capabilities, attributes, and services of a new data infrastructure. In the panel's opinion, CEP's recommendations are consistent with the necessary attributes of a new data infrastructure but are insufficient to form the foundation of this infrastructure. CEP recommended broader access to federal administrative data for statistical purposes and sharing of statistical data resources among the federal statistical agencies, and also recommended that the National Secure Data Service (NSDS) be established, housed within the Department of Commerce, to blend multiple data sources for improved statistics and research. CEP further recommended sharing state-based earnings data for statistical purposes (Commission on Evidence-Based Policymaking, 2017).

The first legislation passed based on CEP's report, the Evidence Act, did not itself create the Commission's proposed NSDS. However, there have been multiple commentaries on alternative organizations that might house NSDS. *Modernizing U.S. Data Infrastructure: Design Considerations for Implementing a National Secure Data Service to Improve Statistics and Evidence Building* (Hart and Potok, 2020) made the case for a new data infrastructure and discussed the establishment, attributes, and organizational options associated with the creation of NSDS. Four approaches were considered:

- Establishing a new agency in the U.S. Department of Commerce;
- Re-tasking an existing agency in the U.S. Department of Commerce;
- Creating a new federally funded research and development center (FFRDC) at NSF; and
- Launching a public-private partnership in a university consortium.

Of these approaches, Potok and Hart recommended the establishment of NSDS as a new federally funded FFRDC at NSF, leveraging the existing legal authorities of the National Center for Science and Engineering Statistics, a principal statistical agency covered by CIPSEA (Hart and Potok, 2020).[35]

The Evidence Act did not mention NSDS but did establish ACDEB, to advise the OMB director and "to review, analyze, and make recommendations on how to promote the use of Federal data for evidence building" (U.S. Congress, 2019, Section 315). ACDEB's Year 1 Report included a vision, framework, and resources associated with NSDS (Advisory Committee on Data for Evidence Building, 2021). At monthly public meetings in 2021, ACDEB discussed the idea of NSDS as an FFRDC located in NSF; however, the Year 1 Report did not comment on the organizational form or the exact organizational placement of NSDS. At ACDEB's meeting in January 2022, NSF announced that the newly established America's DataHub Consortium would serve as a demonstration project for NSDS—sponsored by the National Center for Science and Engineering Statistics, a statistical unit at NSF (Arora, 2022). According to NSF, the "consortium model benefits all levels of government and prioritizes innovation" (Arora, 2022, p. 13). The consortium structure appears to allow flexibility to bring together various organizations and individuals, within and outside of government.

While the organizational structure and location of NSDS remain uncertain, there is an agreement regarding several important issues. First, a National Academies' Committee on National Statistics panel (the National Academies, 2017a), CEP, and ACDEB rejected the idea of establishing a national clearinghouse or data warehouse, due to untenable privacy risks. Any new entity must provide a shared service that permits authorized users to conduct temporary data linkages for exclusively statistical purposes. Second, there is widespread agreement regarding the necessary attributes of NSDS, closely aligning with the eight attributes described by Hart and Potok (2020): transparency and trust, legal authority to protect privacy and confidentiality, independence, legal authority to collect data from agencies, scalable functionality, sustainability, oversight and accountability, and intergovernmental support.

CEP and ACDEB have focused on using federal, state, and local data for evidence building, proposing the establishment of NSDS to bring these data assets together. In the panel's opinion, a comprehensive vision of a new data infrastructure is incomplete without addressing how the blending of private sector data with other data assets might improve the country's understanding of its current situation and prospects. Thus, it is essential to consider the implications of the addition of private sector data assets on organizational options, organization type, and organization placement.

---

[35]This discussion of the placement of NSDS was subsequently expanded to include five more-detailed organizational models (Potok and Hart, 2022).

In sum, the panel's vision of a new data infrastructure involves the addition of important data assets in addition to those currently legislatively endorsed in the Evidence Act (i.e., federal statistical and federal program data), including relevant state, tribal, territory, and local government data assets; relevant private sector data assets; data assets from nonprofits and academic institutions; and crowdsourced or citizen-science data assets.

The panel assumes that, in a new data infrastructure, NSDS will be implemented and will process state, tribal, territory, and local government data as well as federal government data. At the time of this writing, however, the form NSDS will take is not fully evolved, and various organizational models are possible.

Organizational Models to Facilitate Cross-Sector Data Access and Use

The panel's vison of a new data infrastructure should tap assets as necessary, from all sectors of society that produce digital data about the state of the country. Such an infrastructure was not anticipated by the organizational structure of the current federal statistical system. Without organizational change, blended data to improve the current data infrastructure will remain siloed and all too rare. In its vision for a new data infrastructure, the panel assumes that the federal government will eventually implement CEP's recommendations related to an NSDS. Further, the panel assumes that state and local government data will be added to the mission of NSDS. This implies that NSDS will act as an access portal to federal, state, tribal, territory, and local government data assets. But a new data infrastructure also requires a sustainable organizational model for accessing relevant private sector data for common-good statistics, which raises additional challenges.

There are several alternative organizational options for a facility within a new data infrastructure that will produce blended statistics using federal, state, tribal, territory, local, private sector, nonprofit, and academic institution held data as well as crowdsourced data assets. While the panel does not endorse any option, at least one new facility will be required to facilitate the blending of data to create new statistical products, and this entity (or network of entities) will be a key component of a new data infrastructure. For ease of exposition, this report will use the singular terms "facility" or "entity", even though the panel recognizes that there may be multiple coordinated entities. In the panel's judgment, when considering organizational options for the facility, the seven attributes articulated in the vision of a new data infrastructure must be met. These include the privacy-protecting practices and legal reforms necessary to support the infrastructure's authorities, data governance and standards frameworks, and transparency of operations central to its success. Finally, each model facility must be able to access and accommodate federal government statistical and administrative data; state, tribal, territory, and local government data; nonprofits and academic institutions data; private sector data; and crowdsourced or citizen-science data.

In assessing organizational models for a new data infrastructure service, possible iterations of a suitable infrastructure should be considered. CEP and ACDEB have articulated their vision of NSDS, but what are the structural implications of blending state, tribal, territory, local government, and private sector data with data accessible through NSDS? The panel considered seven potential organizational models.

Option 1: NSDS Coordinates Access to All Data Sources

In this vision, NSDS (a combined, comprehensive new entity within the data infrastructure, established with the guidance of ACDEB, with rule-making mandated by the Evidence Act) would have authority over data access from all sectors. This option assumes that NSDS has successfully evolved to provide access to all federal, state, tribal, territory, and local government program and administrative data to be blended with survey and census data for solely statistical purposes. In this model, accessing all data-holder data—including private sector data, data from academic institutions and nonprofits, and crowdsourced or citizen-science data—is included in NSDS's authorities. This model is agnostic to whether the provision of additional data sources for statistical purposes is mandated or incentivized for participant organizations (though, in the panel's opinion, "incentivized" is most realistic). NSDS would develop in partnership with nongovernmental organizations and government agencies to help set access and use protocols. All data-access and privacy-protection procedures would rest on CIPSEA and enhanced legal sanctions.

Option 2: The New Entity Is Placed at a Principal Statistical Agency or a Unit Within Such an Agency

CEP recommended that NSDS be located in the U.S. Department of Commerce as a new principal statical agency leveraging data assets and expertise of the U.S. Census Bureau, BEA, National Institute of Standards and Technology, and the National Oceanic and Atmospheric Administration (Commission on Evidence-Based Policymaking, 2017, Rec. 2-1). CEP added that NSDS "should be situated in such a way as to provide independence sufficient to set strategic priorities distinct from any existing Commerce agency and to operate apart from policy and related offices" (Commission on Evidence-Based Policymaking, 2017, p. 41). In its exploration, the panel was agnostic to where NSDS is housed but—if this route is pursued—the panel recommends that it be housed within a structure with sufficient expertise, funding, and organizational infrastructure to establish and sustain the effort.

Option 3: Authority for the New Entity Is Placed at a New Federally Funded Research and Development Center (FFRDC)

As noted earlier, Hart and Potok (2020) recommended the establishment of NSDS as a new FFRDC at NSF, leveraging the existing legal authorities of the National Center for Science and Engineering Statistics, a principal statistical agency covered by CIPSEA. Other locations are possible if the FFRDC has a federal sponsor and is delegated the authority to provide all NSDS-like services to federal, state, tribal, territory, and local government data holders, as well as to private sector and other data holders. In the panel's view, if this approach is pursued, the FFRDC should have all the rights and responsibilities of a federal statistical agency, coverage under CIPSEA, and access to all data holdings. Such an FFRDC (or FFRDCs) would be expected to develop access protocols in partnership with private-sector organizations, academic partners, and government agencies.

Option 4: A Public-Private Partnership in a University Consortium

Assuming NSDS is established (Option 1), the panel can imagine the creation of a new 501(c)(3) or other 501-section nonprofit organization with the sole purpose of facilitating the secure use of nongovernmental data (including private sector data) for blending with data resources controlled by NSDS. This nonprofit would be governed by a representative body composed from the organizations whose data are accessed by the entity. The panel recommends that such an approach contain a community advisory board to increase accountability to populations whose data are being used. The transparency features of this public-private partnership would include real-time documentation of analyses currently in operation and statistical products being produced. All statistical products from data supplied by the entity could be published for public consumption on the entity's website.

Option 5: NSDS Along with Private Data Compiled Within Given Sectors

This option would rest on a group of sector-specific consortia overseen by NSDS. Each consortium would be a node for blending of sector-specific data with other data pertinent to the industry. Individual data-sharing companies within each sector would not have access to the shared data. However, sharing data with the consortia could be reciprocated by provision of a set of statistical products of value to the sector, with strict privacy protections for all. Each consortium would establish agreements for data sharing that would benefit national statistics. The negotiation of these agreements could be a responsibility of NSDS or the statistical agency whose work could be enhanced with a given sector's data.

Option 6: NSDS Along with Data Gathered by Regional Affiliates

This option is similar to Option 5 but is organized in geographical sets. Such networks might be of interest to activities that affect one another spatially (e.g., healthcare delivery systems or workforce data). Such regional hubs exist and are sharing data (e.g., Cunningham et al., 2022). For example, the Michigan Education Data Center is a secure data clearinghouse that helps researchers use Michigan's education data.[36]

Option 7: A Data Trust

A data trust is a structure whereby data is placed under the control of a board of trustees with a fiduciary responsibility to look after the interests of the beneficiaries. Using a trust offers data holders a greater say in how their data are collected, accessed, and used by others. A data trust goes further than limiting data collecting and access to protect privacy; it promotes the beneficial use of data and ensures benefits are widely felt across society. The data trust form may be overlaid on some of the above structures, like regional or sector options. Trusts must determine who can collect data, who can make decisions about future data collection, who can access data and decide future data access, and who can decide future data use (Ruhaak, 2019). Several of the other options might also take the form of a data trust.

To be successful, any of the models described above will require active engagement with data holders and data users, diverse stakeholders, effective governance, and exemplary transparency. Each model also raises unique questions, including those related to ensuring privacy and security (Box 4-5).

SUMMARY

This chapter discussed the data assets of a 21st century national data infrastructure, including how those assets are sourced and evaluated. Statistics from blended data are central to the panel's vision, and the blending of data has implications on statistical methods, statistical designs, and data-infrastructure capabilities. This chapter also described the privacy and ethical challenges associated with blended data and the organizational structures that could facilitate access and use of multiple data sources.

---

[36]See: https://medc.miedresearch.org/

BOX 4-5
Illustrative Organizational Entity Questions

- To whom will the entity be accountable?
- How will agencies or others retain its services?
- How will the entity's operations affect private sector business models, for example, data brokers?
- Will the entity have authority to impose data or metadata standards? On whom, when, and how?
- How will the entity's many stakeholders interact with it?
- Who will be responsible for selecting the best point on the privacy-accuracy trade-off?
- Will the entity's authority change statistical agencies' existing authority to acquire and use new data assts? How?
- Statistical agencies now have the authority to retain data assets used for statistical purposes—will establishment of the entity change statistical agencies' ability to retain newly acquired data? Under what conditions? How?
- How will the services provided by the entity impact statistical agency survey and program operations and activities? Is the entity only responsible for pilot projects and research, or will it participate in ongoing production of periodic official statistics?
- Will the entity change existing federal statistical research data centers policies, practices, and retention policies? How?
- If new data retention policies are implemented, what are the implications for scientific research? What are the implications for statistical and scientific reproducibility and replicability?

SOURCE: Panel generated.

5

Building a 21st Century National Data Infrastructure Requires Identifying Short- and Medium-Term Activities

While envisioning a coordinated 21st century national data infrastructure is a necessary first step, a vision alone is insufficient. The vision requires accessibility and the use of data for common-good purposes. The assets tapped should include data from the private sector, federal statistical agencies, federal program agencies, state and local government agencies, and other data holders. Such a vision will require trust, data safeguards, legislation, organizational entities, and partnerships that do not yet exist.

This report was written at a time of unusual change. As noted in earlier chapters, the 20th-century infrastructure that produced social and economic statistics was dependent on statistical sampling, self-report surveys and censuses, and the collection, storage, and security of data within secure facilities. Declining participation rates in surveys and censuses have resulted in higher costs and increased risk of flawed statistical estimates. Fortunately, there are a growing number of research and development activities attempting to repair these weaknesses, by combining survey and census data with other data sources. Further, for the first time in decades, the Foundations for Evidence-Based Policymaking Act of 2018 (hereafter, Evidence Act; U.S. Congress, 2019) has allowed the combining of administrative data of federal program agencies with statistical surveys and censuses. However, the Evidence Act *incompletely* implements the vision of the Commission on Evidence-based Policymaking (CEP), whose report was the basis for the legislation.

At the time of this writing, some of the initial building blocks of a 21st century national data infrastructure are already being constructed. Some building blocks implement new laws and regulations, like the Evidence

Act, while others involve an innovative blending of data to answer specific statistical questions. In this chapter, the logical next steps for capitalizing on these initiatives are reviewed. The panel recognizes the importance of being explicit about how its work might be understood in the context of these other ongoing activities.

First, CEP recommended that the protection of data subjects and data holders is a central feature of a new data infrastructure, and the panel fully espouses the same priority (see Chapter 3). However, in the panel's view, merely taking a legal perspective on privacy is inadequate—a more comprehensive view of the ethical foundations of privacy protection is appropriate. Moreover, since eliminating privacy risks is impossible without foregoing uses of data that can greatly benefit the common good, an ethical approach to privacy requires weighing disclosure risks against social benefits. Further, like CEP, the panel holds the view that new technical developments can protect data at the same time that statistical uses can improve the well-being of the population. That is, responsible privacy protection and the use of privacy-enhancing technologies are compatible with expanded statistical uses of data.

Second, CEP recommended that state earnings data and state-collected data acquired by federal departments be shared for evidence-building purposes (Commission on Evidence-Based Policymaking, 2017). The panel shares that judgment because state data could enhance understanding of the current challenges and performances of the job and labor markets. In addition, following the recommendation of the Advisory Committee on Data for Evidence Building ([ACDEB] Advisory Committee on Data for Evidence Building, 2021), the panel advises that increased sharing of other state- and local-government administrative data could be useful for social and economic statistics (e.g., digital data on criminal incidents) and could benefit state and local governments in other ways. All the logic that supports the blending of federal administrative data with statistical survey data to construct better statistical information applies to state and local government data as well.

Third, CEP is silent on statistical uses of private sector data for the benefit of common-good statistics. Private sector data were not part of the scope of the evidence-building charge to the Commission. In contrast, as discussed in earlier chapters, the panel sees the merit of blending private sector data with other government sources of administrative and statistical data to produce more granular, timely, and relevant information about the economy and society.

Fourth, CEP recommended establishing a National Secure Data Service (NSDS) for the creation of statistical information for evidence building. The panel, too, sees the value of such a service. Beyond evidence building, the panel sees a further value of NSDS for facilitating the blending of diverse data sources from the private sector. Alternatively, as noted in Chapter 4, a separate facility could be built to facilitate new statistical information from the blending of private sector and government-sector data. Thus, in the panel's view, there are multiple possible ways forward in terms of building a structure to support a new data infrastructure.

Fifth, the Evidence Act gives statistical agencies access to federal administrative data, unless specifically prohibited by law. While this is an important advance in improving statistical information, additional changes in laws and regulations are needed to permit the expanded use of federal, state, and local government administrative data for purely statistical uses. Engaging sovereign tribes and territories to access administrative data from their governments require a separate approach.

The panel does not attempt to identify each of the sequential steps necessary to achieve a new data infrastructure—many of the methods to achieve the panel's vision are feasible but dependent on building support among key stakeholders. Instead, the panel has identified short-term and medium-term activities that could be performed to discern the best ways for the United States to progress toward the panel's full vision of a new data infrastructure. Later steps in achieving the vision will be dependent on:

- Further legislation to implement CEP recommendations;
- The technical and statistical outcomes of the many pilot projects now ongoing;
- How private sector stakeholders and other nongovernmental data holders evolve in their contributions to national statistics that promote the common good;
- Future refinement of NSDS vision;
- How data sharing under NSDS evolves; and
- Concurrent changes in federal statistical agencies.

In considering its vision, the panel assumes that legislative changes will have important implications for private sector incentives for sharing data to improve statistical information. Legal reform will likely also inform organizational and governance features of a new data infrastructure. Similarly, budgetary support for the infrastructure will be established.

This chapter is organized around the same seven attributes of a new data infrastructure described in Chapter 3. The panel offers some short-term and medium-term tasks associated with each key attribute and the organizations/partnerships of a new data infrastructure; these tasks are summarized in Table 5-1.

ATTRIBUTE 1: SAFEGUARDS AND ADVANCED PRIVACY-ENHANCING PRACTICES TO MINIMIZE POSSIBLE INDIVIDUAL HARM

All parts of society—the private sector, nonprofit organizations, academia, the government, and the U.S. public—have learned how disclosure of private information can result in harm. Harm is often more acute in vulnerable communities. The panel envisions a turnaround: the use of the same data for the common good of society. To achieve this vision, a new data infrastructure must, in the panel's judgment, have high levels of data protection, trust, and equity designed into its core. In short, building a new data infrastructure that mitigates the risk of individual harm and maximizes widespread and equitable benefits is required for its legitimacy.

Notions of privacy are one example of concerns connected to more basic values (Beauchamp and Childress, 2001). The values that guide the actions of a new data infrastructure call for an orientation to the data subject. First, how are the digital data connected to data subjects affecting their lives? Second, there are underlying issues of "autonomy"—the ability of individuals to make their own decisions. In the panel's view, a new data infrastructure must recognize the nature of informed consent by the data subject. Third, there is concern about "beneficence"—to what extent will the data be used to produce good outcomes for the data subject? Finally, there is a focus on human dignity—are the uses of a new data infrastructure conducted in a manner that is respectful of the data subjects? These underlying values are important for a new data infrastructure because they are related to the development of trust between those whose data resides in the infrastructure and the outcomes of that infrastructure.

As noted in Chapter 3, societal trust begins with legitimacy as sanctioned by credible institutions—formal assurance, through law and technology, that data will be safeguarded, secured, protected, and used responsibly and ethically for approved statistical purposes. But, in the panel's judgment, this is not enough. Community-oriented legitimacy is also essential. Mandates preserve privacy and protect confidentiality. Transparent procedures allow data holders to understand how their data are being used, by whom, and for what societal benefit. Policies and principles inform day-to-day practices and underpin effective controls related to data access and use. Practices implement advanced protective cybersecurity measures, facilitate shared computing approaches that preserve privacy and protect the confidentiality, and mandate transparency and stakeholder engagement. Effective monitoring, enforcement, evaluation, and accountability mitigate risk and strengthen trust.

In the panel's view, all future visions of a new data infrastructure need a stronger set of safeguards to assure that data will not be used to harm any individual or data subject. The panel notes that the societal benefits of statistical information do not have to come at the price of the increased threat to privacy and confidentiality if this threat is effectively and proactively addressed. Statistical analyses of existing data resources can provide information about the well-being of those in society and can contribute to the common good. Attention to the broader ecosystem of data can also highlight data inequities that can unduly harm certain communities. The panel's vision of a new data infrastructure proposes little new data collection but instead suggests the expanded and responsible use of existing data to produce better information about critical features of society.

Oversight functions with some authority to evaluate the performance of data protections have been introduced usefully in other countries (see Chapter 3). Some countries have demonstrated ways to be more transparent about their practices, operations, and activities. It is the panel's opinion that trust in a new data infrastructure requires such transparency.

Currently, federal data resources held by statistical agencies, once collected, are protected by laws prohibiting their use for nonstatistical or inappropriate purposes. What is largely absent, however, are features that include active participation by those whose data are held by the agencies. In the panel's judgment, active engagement of data holders, subjects, and other stakeholders is needed, in the development of data-infrastructure policies that affect them. With such a formal partnership, the building of trust might be more easily achieved.

As a short-term task, the panel suggests that the United States begin dialogues and convenings to discuss practical vehicles for building a privacy-protecting culture, as an integral part of a new data infrastructure. The dialogues should take the perspectives of both the data subject and the data holder. The values underlying the proposed safeguard practices of a new data infrastructure should be made clear. The panel supports CEP's evocation of the principle of "humility"—the notion that data use must not be driven exclusively by the analysts but should involve the concerns of data subjects. In the short term, these dialogues with data subjects and data holders should envision and evaluate alternative structures and practices that would continue the value-based devotion to a data-subject orientation, while incorporating new privacy-protecting tools created over time. These convenings would establish *mechanisms* to engage all stakeholders regarding the data-safeguard prerequisites necessary to build trust. Convenings could also help develop a strategy for ensuring data safeguards are *communicated* effectively and transparently to data subjects, data holders, and other important stakeholders. Finally, the convenings could establish *technical specifications* of privacy-preserving and confidentiality-protecting designs.

The medium-term tasks could focus on the establishment of *organizational* mechanisms for oversight that safeguards privacy and confidentiality procedures. The oversight mechanisms and procedures could become features of existing advisory structures of statistical agencies. The development and sharing of relevant procedures, processes, and practices for protecting the rights of data subjects and data holders could also result.

ATTRIBUTE 2: STATISTICAL USES ONLY, FOR COMMON-GOOD INFORMATION, WITH STATISTICAL AGGREGATES FREELY SHARED WITH ALL

Data on individuals and economic units can be used for administrative procedures and/or statistical purposes (see Chapter 3). The administrative use of data regarding the attributes of an individual can affect that individual by granting or denying that person some benefit. The Evidence Act noted that administrative uses of data require access to identifiable data on an individual and have "administrative, regulatory, law enforcement, adjudicatory, or other purposes that affect the rights, privileges and benefits of a particular identifiable respondent…" (U.S. Congress, 2019, 44 USC 3561). Statistical uses may act on the same set of data but, instead of producing actions on individuals, produce aggregated, estimated, or modeled information. CEP focused attention on the use of statistical practices to evaluate government programs—evidence building.

Both CEP and the panel noted that data collected for administrative purposes can be valuable when blended with data collected for statistical purposes only. Note that federal statistical agencies have missions limited exclusively to statistical uses of data. The Evidence Act granted statistical agencies the right to acquire federal-agency administrative data for statistical purposes unless such use is prohibited by another law.

The panel expects that, under full implementation of the Evidence Act, statistical agencies will gain experience blending federal administrative data with their survey and census data. Data blending experiences could build a culture in which the distinction between administrative and statistical uses of data are better clarified by stakeholder groups. This distinction is important in building societal trust regarding the benefits of a new data infrastructure, relative to any risks that may exist. In the panel's summation, an important goal is to clearly frame the distinction between "statistical uses" and "administrative uses" of data in public discourse.

Ongoing pilot projects at federal statistical agencies and among academic researchers can illustrate the production of improved statistical information by the blending of data from multiple sources. Statistical uses of data can produce a much more favorable benefit-threat balance than can administrative uses, though it is unclear whether the public understands this distinction. Public support for a new data infrastructure could be enhanced by a widespread understanding of this difference.

In the short term, it would be useful to make the value of new statistical information more publicly visible via the internet and other accessible media. Such communication might build a wider understanding of the value of a new data infrastructure for solely statistical uses. A description explaining the autonomy of a new data infrastructure, in terms of freedom from political interference, could also contribute to public acceptance.

Similarly, stakeholder convenings could be useful to mount a dialogue about the best way to describe a new data infrastructure's statistical products, distinguishing statistical uses from uses that threaten abuse of individuals' data. Another short-term task could involve monitoring the outcomes of the newly introduced Standard Application Process (SAP), which is when blended data are used to produce new research products (Marten, 2022). By definition, those research products are statistical uses of data. A communications campaign that alerts the public about the value of such research could be useful.

In the medium term, work on this "statistical uses" attribute could guide reform efforts for the regulatory environment of a new data infrastructure. In the new legislation, the treatment of "statistical uses" in contrast to "administrative uses" is important to build the trust of data subjects and data holders in a new data infrastructure.

ATTRIBUTE 3: MOBILIZATION OF RELEVANT DIGITAL DATA ASSETS, BLENDED IN STATISTICAL AGGREGATES TO PROVIDE BENEFITS TO DATA HOLDERS, WITH SOCIETAL BENEFITS PROPORTIONATE TO POSSIBLE COSTS AND RISKS

The variety and volume of the potential data assets available to a new data infrastructure are large. While the 20th-century data infrastructure relied on the physical movement of data from one holder to another or relatively small amounts of digital data, the size of current and future datasets useful to society dictates that they must be accessed digitally from the data holder or owner—these datasets are too big to move from place to place. Although it is a significant change from existing practices, this shift—from collecting data, moving them to the statistical agency's facility, and processing them there, to data access and processing at the data owner's facility—offers many potential benefits. This "distributed data-connecting" model is now being piloted (see Chapter 4). Monitoring and learning from such pilots are short-term tasks that can provide valuable insights into the capabilities and challenges of this new approach.

How should data be accessed in a new data infrastructure? First, the panel notes the recent implementation of the Evidence Act's SAP by the Interagency Council on Statistical Policy (ICSP) and the Office of Management and Budget's (OMB's) Statistical and Science Policy Branch (Marten,

2022). The SAP allows qualified researchers and others to apply, become qualified, and obtain approval to access *existing* federal statistical agency data, and it appears to be the primary mechanism for such access. Under the SAP, researcher access will generally, but not always, be through federal statistical research data centers (FSRDCs)—a network of 31 sites across the United States that have expanded the insights obtained from data through original analyses that must be made publicly available. FSRDCs are university-statistical agency collaborations that also offer researchers support in understanding and accessing data, as well as both physical and virtual access to data. While CEP Recommendation 2-8 focused on researchers (Commission on Evidence-Based Policymaking, 2017), the Evidence Act and ICSP propose that federal agencies, the Congressional Budget Office, state, local, and tribal governments, researchers, and other individuals use the SAP to apply for access to confidential statistical data assets for purposes of developing evidence (Federal Register, 2022). Under these proposals, other executive-branch agencies or units could also utilize the SAP to accept applications for access to their confidential data assets. Monitoring the implementation and effectiveness of the SAP as an access tool, distinct from the value of the resulting research (Attribute 2, short-term task) could provide important insights into the SAP's ability to serve a broader user base than just researchers. Medium-term tasks include monitoring if the SAP is used as a data-access tool for the National Science Foundation's (NSF's) America's Data Hub Consortium (ADC).[1]

As mentioned previously, the Evidence Act has provided broader statutory authority for combining data from federal administrative and statistical agencies, unless prohibited by law. The Evidence Act did not, however, implement CEP recommendations related to providing access to important state administrative data. Advisory Committee on Data for Evidence Building did recommend legislation broadening access to state data (2021) and, more recently, the ACDEB Subcommittee on Governance, Accountability, and Transparency recommended use cases that access, link, and analyze federal, state, and local government data assets (Cutshall and Lane, 2022). Use cases focused on education and workforce data, health statistics, and labor-market activity. In the panel's opinion, these pilots are a necessary step forward in demonstrating the value of a new data infrastructure, as well as identifying barriers and useful data-governance frameworks.

CEP's recommendations, the Evidence Act, and ACDEB's proposals lead the panel to conclude that the first data assets to be acquired should be those of federal program agencies, followed by those of federally funded state programs for which access is legally permitted. During this period,

---

[1]See: https://beta.nsf.gov/science-matters/americas-datahub-consortium-seeing-and-understanding-entire-elephant?utm_medium=email&utm_source=govdelivery

---

BOX 5-1
Properties of First Additions to a New Data Infrastructure
for Statistical Purposes

- Data are necessary, minimized for uses and benefits are proportional to costs and risks.
- Legal/regulatory barriers are nonexistent, minor, or can be addressed promptly.
- Coverage, data quality, and data limitations are well documented and understood.
- Statistical system lead organization is identified and has the necessary resources to direct the project.
- Data holder is engaged, supportive, has necessary skills, and is willing to participate.
- Intended use demonstrates the benefits and power of blended data to address issues of national importance.

SOURCE: Panel generated.

---

dialogue with private sector and other nongovernmental data holders can sharpen mutual understanding of the value of data sharing for national statistical purposes. In addition, in the short term, the activities of the ICSP working group on the use of private sector data (see Chapter 2) should be monitored.

In the panel's judgment, additional decision criteria are needed to decide the order by which data assets should be added to a new data infrastructure. To establish data-asset priorities, it is useful to consider criteria that can be used to rate various types of data assets. To stimulate discussion, the panel suggests the criteria in Box 5-1.

In the panel's vision of a new data infrastructure, NSDS or its demonstration pilots,[2] like America's DataHub Consortium (ADC), will have access to federal agency program data that are not explicitly prohibited for such statistical uses. In the panel's opinion, those data should be the priority for expanded statistical uses. Among those are data assets that offer full coverage of important target populations (e.g., Medicare, Supplemental Nutrition Assistance Program) and those with standardized and stable data documentation. Broadening access to data assets that are already being used by statistical agencies may be easier than attempting to use the data for different purposes, which requires the re-negotiation of existing agreements. First, newly acquired data assets should have immediate utility, in terms of

---

[2]The CHIPS and Science Act (PL 117-167) was signed into law on August 9, 2022. It allocates funding for an unnamed demonstration project to inform establishment of NSDS.

improving statistical products and research productivity. Next, the current data holder should be able to quickly acquire the technical skills necessary to permit data access by NSDS. Ideally, the first newly acquired data assets, when blended with other data, would produce statistical information and research products that would provide new insights into the functioning of the economy or society at large.

In short, in the panel's judgment, the first new data assets to be added to those currently used for statistical purposes should be easily acquired and demonstrate the value of blending data from diverse sources for an increased understanding of national issues.

In building a 21st century data infrastructure, early success may come first from integrating data that are relatively easily available, demonstrating the utility of improved statistical information of national importance, and constructing effective partnerships for necessary legal changes. (Conclusion 5-1)

In the panel's opinion, evaluations of existing efforts to access state government data for statistical purposes should begin as soon as feasible, as in some of the use cases proposed by ACDEB (e.g., Cutshell and Lane, 2022). These data could build upon existing federal survey and administrative data. The panel expects, as did CEP, that state and local government program data from federally funded programs be the first to be accessed when permitted by law. However, the panel acknowledges that the multiple jurisdictions involved may pose complications greater than those presented by the relatively small number of federal agencies collecting societally relevant data.

A key feature of a new data infrastructure is the reciprocation principle: data holders that share their data will benefit from new statistical information useful to their operations. While the panel expects that many jurisdictions will learn from comparing their statistics to those of other areas, some jurisdictions will suggest new statistical products that require development. In the panel's view, in the short term, attention should be paid to actively learning about how jurisdictions could benefit from sharing their data for statistical purposes. While short-term efforts will pay large dividends, the panel expects that accessing state- and local-government data resources will require more time.

In the short-term, statistical agencies will continue to acquire and use private sector and other nongovernmental data for statistical purposes. In the panel's view, these initiatives should be closely monitored by agency decisionmakers, and lessons learned should be shared across the statistical system. Early "data-connecting" pilots that will access and process data at data holders' sites are precursors of a future access strategy, and a key, specified feature of NSDS. In the panel's view, understanding the capabilities, expertise, and challenges associated with this approach is necessary and will be informative.

Finally, not only data holders will benefit from data sharing. In the panel's judgment, societal benefits should be proportionate to the possible costs and risks of acquiring and using a data asset. In the short term, ongoing initiatives must be examined to identify associated benefits and costs. In the panel's judgment, it would be useful to convene a group to evaluate various methods for documenting and possibly quantifying the benefits and costs of acquiring and using data. In some cases, to incentivize state and local data holders, a new data infrastructure may have to help cover the costs incurred by data holders.

Medium-term tasks include accessing using federal administrative data as well as state and local data, implementing "data connecting" prototypes into a true statistical production system, and evaluating ADC's use of the SAP as a possible access tool. Learning from these existing efforts will help clarify and refine data governance, access, and use policies, rules, and procedures.

ATTRIBUTE 4: REFORMED LEGAL AUTHORITIES PROTECTING ALL PARTIES' INTERESTS

In the panel's view, to create new statistical information valuable to the country, data with the fewest regulatory or logistical impediments could be accessed first by a new data infrastructure. Next, data that have potential value but have technical or logistic impediments should be acquired. Finally, changes in regulations or laws must occur before certain data can become part of a new data infrastructure. Figure 5-1 illustrates the basic steps of this transition.

A new data infrastructure will utilize new technologies to access data without possessing them. This is a specified feature of NSDS which, in the panel's view, is likely to be a key feature of the success of a new data infrastructure—assuming that the operational requisites to access federal program agency data occur.

There are logical sequences to further regulatory reform. One of the most important CEP recommendations that were not included in the Evidence Act was the establishment of NSDS. Advisory Committee on Data for Evidence Building (2021) affirmed the need for NSDS, and the former co-chairs of the Evidence Commission encouraged U.S. Congress to include the NSDS Act in the conferenced version of the U.S. Innovation and Competition Act,[3] but at the time of this writing, no legislation has been

---

[3]See the co-chairs' letter to Congress: http://www.datacoalition.org/wp-content/uploads/2021/11/CEP-Co-Chair-Letter-re-NSDS-11-30-2021.pdf

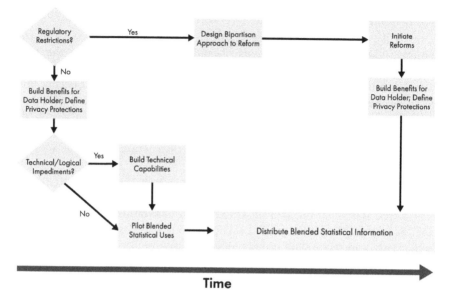

FIGURE 5-1 Steps in building a regulatory environment supporting private sector data sharing for national statistical purposes.
SOURCE: Panel generated.

enacted. Clarity regarding the legislative prospects for establishing NSDS should be a short-term priority, in the panel's opinion.[4]

The Evidence Act authorized the use of federal program administrative data by statistical agencies and units, but OMB rulemaking and regulations must be enacted to guide these agencies. The panel's vision assumes that, over the short term, the blending of federal program administrative data with survey and census data will take place. CEP also recommended access to quarterly earnings data held by states, and state-collected data acquired by federal departments. Legislative and regulatory priorities regarding these CEP recommendations should be a short-term priority, in the panel's judgment.

In the panel's view, a first step could be to catalog all the state regulatory features that affect data sharing, especially those that might affect blending with private sector data. Any regulatory reform activities to permit such sharing of state and local government data solely for statistical purposes

---

[4]As noted in Chapters 2 and earlier in this chapter, the CHIPS and Science Act (PL 117-167) was signed into law on August 9th, 2022. While this legislation calls for a demonstration project for NSDS, it did not formally establish a fully-functioning NSDS.

are also important short-term activities. These activities would naturally be part of any legislative or regulatory action that follows the existing Evidence Act prescriptions for data sharing. In addition, other legislation, for example, the proposals for data synchronization[5] would logically receive actions, permitting sharing of specified IRS business data among the Bureau of Economic Analysis, the Bureau of Labor Statistics, and the U.S. Census Bureau, for statistical purposes. In the short term, it would be useful for an expert group to consider legislative proposals that could incentivize data holders to share their data with a new data infrastructure. Such proposals for incentives could include legal liability protection against legal actions directly related to the act of data sharing, or possible tax incentives.

Medium-term activities, according to the panel's vision, should concentrate on reforms that involve private sector data. These might be the development of regional or sector-based hubs of shared data, permitting access to statistical information by NSDS. A data hub might constitute a new institution—a new private-public partnership. Any of these options will require careful, trust-building activities among the various sectors whose data will form part of a new infrastructure. During these activities, drafting of the legislative language to underlie the new entity facilitating sharing of private sector data should occur.

ATTRIBUTE 5: GOVERNANCE FRAMEWORK AND STANDARDS EFFECTIVELY SUPPORTING OPERATIONS

Much of the governance framework and the definition of standards necessary for a new data infrastructure (see Chapter 4) will necessarily follow the reform of the regulatory environment described above. The components of a data-governance framework involve a set of formal processes and procedures that implement the underlying principles of the infrastructure (Box 5-2).

The components in Box 5-2 have a logical sequencing, which could guide the short-term activities to implement a new data infrastructure. The choice of which type of governance body with which authorities best fits the United States naturally precedes the identification of standards, policies, and procedures. In the panel's vision, statistical agencies play a prominent role in these discussions.

In the short term, the panel recommends that potential data-sharing organizations could be convened to foster a partnership informed by the concerns and standard practices of said organizations. Documentation of

---

[5]In 2021, the U.S. Department of Treasury proposed changes to allow data synchronization: https://home.treasury.gov/system/files/131/General-Explanations-FY2022.pdf, pp. 101–102. In a letter to Secretary Yellen, the American Economic Association endorsed this approach: https://www.aeaweb.org/content/file?id=14973

BOX 5-2
Data Governance Components

- Data-governance bodies and structures. The structures often focus on specific aspects of governance: strategic, tactical, and operational.
- Necessary authorities to access, link, and use data.
- Standards and guidance that facilitate interoperability, uniformity, and reuse.
- Policies, rules, and procedures that govern data acquisition, access, use, management, and protection.
- Processes and capabilities that touch data, like data exchange and data transformation.
- Platforms, technologies, and tools to access data from diverse platforms, perform necessary linkages, and conduct analysis while preserving privacy and protecting confidentiality.

SOURCE: Panel generated.

---

current procedures for accessing data within data-sharing organizations could begin at these convenings, including documentation of decision-making procedures for granting access, both internal and external to the organization. The convenings could catalog the variety of software platforms used by potential data-sharing organizations and could assemble information on the metadata practices of various organizations. The convenings could also identify priorities for standards development. Finally, the convenings could generate reports suggesting standards that could be incorporated as part of a new data infrastructure. In a parallel set of activities, drafts of data-governance guidelines could be developed, for review by diverse stakeholder groups.

In the medium term, guidelines could be integrated into drafts of key legislative changes, so that the governance procedures and practices would have the force of statutes.

In the panel's judgment, relevant stakeholders should be convened to begin developing standards in response to the identified data-infrastructure priorities. A group should be charged with establishing governance roles and responsibilities.

ATTRIBUTE 6: TRANSPARENCY TO THE PUBLIC REGARDING ANALYTICAL OPERATIONS USING THE DATA INFRASTRUCTURE

One of the critical design decisions for a new data infrastructure is choosing which transparency-building approaches best fit U.S. society, with its diverse interest groups. Extreme transparency would permit anyone at any given time to answer several questions:

- Which data are currently being accessed in statistical operations?
- Which data are being blended?
- What are the informational goals of blending?
- What purposes will be served and what benefits will be realized by the statistical products produced?
- How will the statistical products be distributed?

Wide dissemination of answers to these questions could create a level of transparency that might help to alleviate fears of data misuse and its associated harm to certain subpopulations. Dissemination could also raise awareness about the uses of data for the common good, which could bolster support of a new data infrastructure.

Chapter 3 reviewed various approaches for building transparency into the operations of a new data infrastructure, including a variety of structural features that could provide insight into the operations of the infrastructure. Other countries have employed alternative formal mechanisms:

- An ombudsperson to mediate the public's, data subjects', or data holders' concerns with the organizations using the infrastructure;
- An information commissioner;
- A multi-person commission or other institution; and
- A Review Council that regulates data sharing.

In the panel's opinion, all of these mechanisms gain their influence when they reveal to society how data are being used. The key stakeholders in transparency efforts are data subjects (who are described by records in the infrastructure), data holders (who are giving access to their datasets), and the general public (whose interests should be served by the statistical products of the new infrastructure).

Formal transparency-building structures could act on concerns about the failure to achieve a new data infrastructure's mission to serve the common good. The various roles and structures implemented by other countries comprise ways to create a forum for the expression of those concerns. Legislative and regulatory reform initiatives are likely to incorporate the chosen definitions of roles or bodies created to act on data-infrastructure concerns or failures.

In the short term, the panel recommends increased public discussion of the types of oversight likely to enhance the credibility and trustworthiness of a new data infrastructure. CEP held a series of public meetings across the country to seek such input.[6] In the panel's opinion, more such gatherings might inform alternative structures and practices that could build meaningful transparency into a new data infrastructure.

Transparency also involves taking the perspective of the stakeholders seeking to understand the operations of infrastructure. Discussions with stakeholders could identify communication priorities and evaluate alternative bodies and roles (e.g., ombuds, oversight bodies) whose purpose is informing society about the infrastructure's current state or well-being. In the short term, discussions with stakeholders could produce a digest of the various ways data are currently curated, protected, and preserved, and could identify communication priorities.

In the medium term, the panel recommends that a communication strategy be implemented to respond to stakeholders' priorities. Community oversight of a new data infrastructure needs to be one of the infrastructure's key features. The ideas generated in the short-term stakeholder outreach must become part of the regulatory reform deliberations.

ATTRIBUTE 7: STATE-OF-THE-ART PRACTICES FOR ACCESS, STATISTICAL, COORDINATION, AND COMPUTATIONAL ACTIVITIES; CONTINUOUSLY IMPROVED TO EFFICIENTLY CREATE INCREASINGLY SECURE AND USEFUL INFORMATION

Earlier chapters in this report noted a large number of ongoing pilot projects, each of which is combining datasets not originally designed to be combined. All of these pilots are seeking more timely, accurate, and granular statistical information that can inform decisionmakers and the public. The pilot projects are addressing the challenges of diverse data structures, metadata standards, and regulatory restrictions. In addition, the pilot projects are necessarily innovating in terms of the technical aspects of data access and aggregation, and statistical estimation issues.

Certain high-velocity technological developments are relevant to a new data infrastructure. Cybersecurity approaches are undergoing rapid development. The role of encryption in data sharing is changing rapidly. The size of datasets has grown so large as to make infeasible their movement from one site to another. Hence, software approaches to allow remote users to

---

[6]For a description of CEP's public engagement, see: https://bipartisanpolicy.org/wp-content/uploads/2019/03/CEP-FAQs.pdf

access data where those data exist are increasingly being developed. The design of NSDS, as conceived by CEP, assumes no data warehousing, but real-time access, blending, and construction of statistics from multiple data sets simultaneously.[7] Such approaches should profit from continuous improvements in technologies supporting multiserver and multiple-cloud use.

Many of the innovations in cybersecurity and multisite computing are taking place in private sector information firms (e.g., Microsoft Azure, Amazon EC2). The level of investment in these firms greatly exceeds that of organizations actively producing statistical products from social and economic data. Concerns about the ability of federal statistical agencies to acquire cutting-edge technical talent to support the role of the federal government in a new data infrastructure were noted in Chapter 3. It was also noted that new partnerships between the private sector, the academic sector, and the federal government might explore new approaches to this challenge. Current pilot projects are underway, involving e-commerce data for measurement of price and quantity for retail trade statistics, which place highly secure aggregation software within the protected cloud of the firm. In the panel's vision, a similar approach could involve pre-vetted software "behind the firewall" of NSDS or the federal statistical agency producing aggregate statistical products for dissemination to the public. New partnership models seem important for the success of a new data infrastructure.

In the short term, if these pilots continue, agencies will develop new approaches to data access, matching, merging, and computation. Building a community of practice for such data blending could catalyze progress on the technical-skill base. The panel suggests targeted, periodic meetings in which tools, techniques, and skill sets are described and evaluated. Professional associations (e.g., the American Statistical Association) often serve such purposes. The Federal Committee on Statistical Methodology holds periodic conferences where such work could be showcased.

Also in the short term, the panel advises wider discussions about the need to educate staff on new procedures necessary for a new data infrastructure. Data access, transmission, curation, processing, computation, and statistical forms will all undergo continuous change over the coming years. Federal statistical agencies, other public-sector entities, and infrastructure-participating entities need a new generation of technical staff that can function across these various procedures. Staying current with new developments will require continuous updating of skills. Institutionalizing ongoing learning as a norm will necessitate additional training in the short

---

[7]Note that this design is also compatible with the notion of data minimization—that only the data necessary for a given purpose are acquired to fulfill that purpose—as another tool to reduce risk to data subjects and data holders.

term. Academic institutions and other key stakeholders can participate in these dialogues.

Over the medium term, in the panel's view, new partnerships need to be formed between existing statistical operations and organizations with the skills needed to create and maintain a new data infrastructure. Currently, private sector internet-information enterprises are investing in the development of new tools for cybersecurity, data access, and privacy protection. In the panel's opinion, these investments will create new tools and practices that can benefit a new data infrastructure. Hence, collaboration across the public and private sectors will be an important vehicle for the evolution of the infrastructure.

NEW PARTNERSHIPS MUST BE FORMED

Alternative organizational models for a new data infrastructure were reviewed in Chapter 4. This section assumes that NSDS will be established and will provide access to federal, state, and local government data for federal statistical and research purposes. In the panel's opinion, the next component to design, build, and operate should be an organizational form to facilitate access to private sector data.

Three paths exist in terms of accessing private sector data: (1) whether access to private sector data for blending should be voluntary or mandated;[8] (2) whether NSDS adds private sector data to its purview or whether private sector data reside in one or more separate entities; and (3) whether the federal statistical system alone governs the entity/entities accessing private sector data, or whether governance involves a new public-private partnership. If NSDS becomes the direct portal for access to private sector data for national statistical purposes, fewer steps are necessary. If one or more new entities are established for accessing or blending private sector data, they must be designed, evaluated, and built. For ease of exposition in the discussion that follows, the new entity or entities are simply referred to as the "entity", without assuming whether there will be one or more entities.

As reviewed in Chapter 4, the new feature common to all organizational options for an entity is a technical staff with the skills needed to develop and maintain the entity. Staff would need to be highly skilled in the curation of data for statistical purposes, as well as in safeguarding and managing data access and use. Staff would need skills specific to building software for remote access to curated data and for interacting with oversight bodies. In the panel's view, short-term work involves designing the specific technical services to be provided by NSDS and other important data-infrastructure entities, like the FSRDC network.

---

[8]The panel assumes that access will be voluntary.

Dialogue between governmental and private sector data holders is important in the early days of creating an entity. In the federal government, both executive- and legislative-branch involvement are important because the entity will either be an integral part of NSDS or be in frequent interaction with NSDS. With such options inevitably come unique legal and regulatory implications.

Over the short term, the lessons learned from experience with the NSF-sponsored ADC initiative will become clearer. This model of sector- and region-based data sharing for research purposes may inform the features of a new entity involving the sharing of private sector data.

Early in the development of an entity, the panel assumes that other features of NSDS will become fully formed through legislation and regulation. Finally, all the necessary data agreements between the new entity and NSDS will be drafted and vetted by leaders of private sector entities as well as government officials.

In the short term, it will also be useful, in the panel's opinion, to clarify the roles and responsibilities of the entity, including the services and capabilities of the FSRDC network. A bipartisan, multi-sector dialogue about how best to manage and govern private sector data for national statistical purposes could have important implications for the organization of a new data infrastructure.

In the panel's vision, medium-term tasks would involve piloting the operations of the new entity and interacting with initial private sector enterprises involved with those pilots. New pilots could usefully build on the experience, lessons learned, and challenges highlighted in the initial pilots. Scaling up the operations of an entity to handle multiple enterprises in various sectors, to provide access to diverse kinds of data for different statistical program types, will highlight additional challenges and issues. However, this scaling up will also identify benefits for private sector data holders that can be used to incentivize broader data sharing. Scaling up data-blending pilot projects to test data-service capabilities and responsiveness will provide important insights and identify issues that may need to be addressed. If a new entity other than NSDS is given responsibility for private sector data blending, a new or refined governance framework may be needed.

The panel anticipates that the sustainability of a new entity will be enhanced by forging a cooperative relationship between that entity, data holders, and key stakeholders. The reciprocal nature of the relationship could be key. Figure 5-2 shows two paths for the entity's relationship with a data holder—a data-protection and data-sharing path, and an information-enrichment path. Participating data holders enjoy the benefits of state-of-the-art privacy protection and new information products that can help their businesses. Enhanced privacy-protection expertise could easily migrate from data accessed for statistical uses to a data holder's entire enterprise.

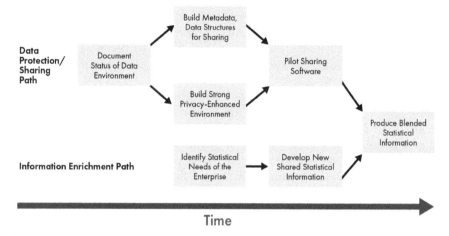

FIGURE 5-2 Entity actions to build partnerships with data-sharing private sector data holders.
SOURCE: Panel generated.

In that way, a new entity hardens the country's private sector data against cybersecurity breaches and inadvertent re-identification of data. Dialogue between the entity's leadership and data holders would guide either path. Design and piloting work building a strong privacy-protecting environment could benefit data holders and the U.S. public. In the panel's vision, all new information products would be publicly available and a large overlap in information needs is expected among data sharers.

SUMMARY

There is much to do. A proposed new data infrastructure will build a coordinated ecosystem of data from all parts of society, for the benefit of the whole society. Table 5-1 presents a terse overview of the short- and medium-term tasks discussed above, for building a 21st century national data infrastructure for social and economic data, and the research said infrastructure could facilitate.

This report began with evidence that available data are insufficient to provide the United States with statistical information on critical societal features. The tools of the 20th century are not well suited to the challenges of the 21st century. At the same time, society is awash in digital data that could be used for larger societal benefits.

The panel presented a vision that moves the country toward a 21st century national data infrastructure, by mobilizing information for the

TABLE 5-1 Short- and Medium-Term Tasks for a 21st Century National Data Infrastructure

Attribute of New Data Infrastructure	Short-Term Tasks	Medium-Term Tasks
Safeguards and advanced privacy-enhancing practices	1. Establish mechanisms to engage stakeholders (including data subjects, data holders, and other responsible organizations) regarding data-safeguard prerequisites for building trust 2. Develop a strategy to ensure key data safeguards are communicated effectively and transparently 3. Establish technical specifications of privacy-preserving and confidentiality-protecting designs	1. Propose community and data-holder council to ensure data subjects' interests are respected 2. Publish safeguard procedures and mechanisms 3. Publish privacy/confidentiality procedures 4. Establish external council for safeguard oversight
Statistical uses only, for common-good information	1. Use pilots to promote wider understanding of "statistical uses" 2. Convene stakeholders to determine how to best describe new statistical products and distinguish them from privacy-threatening initiatives 3. Monitor outcomes of the new Standard Access Process (SAP) for research uses of shared data, to demonstrate value of research as a "statistical use" of data 4. Launch communication campaign about the value of data	1. Improve legislative language describing value of statistical uses versus administrative uses, to build data-subject and data-holder trust

continued

TABLE 5-1 Continued

Attribute of New Data Infrastructure	Short-Term Tasks	Medium-Term Tasks
Mobilization of all relevant national digital data assets	1. Seek researcher input regarding SAP implementation as an access tool 2. Monitor activities of ICSP working group on private sector data 3. Monitor "data-connecting" pilots collecting data at the data holder's site 4. Publish criteria for prioritizing new data assets 5. Convene a group to evaluate methods for documenting and possibly quantifying benefits and costs 6. Identify blended statistics generated by statistical agencies, document and possibly quantify benefits and costs 7. Monitor pilot projects for blended federal/state/local data 8. Consider feasibility and means of covering some data-holder costs associated with data sharing	1. Monitor Data Hub's use of SAP as an application, approval, and access tool 2. Access federal program/administrative data for statistical purposes; document benefits and costs 3. Access state, territory, tribal and local data for statistical purposes; document benefits and costs 4. Implement "data-connecting" learnings and technologies into statistical program production 5. Clarify data-governance access and use policies, rules, and procedures incorporating learnings from short-term activities
Reformed legal authorities	1. Legislation establishes the design, authorities, and funding for NSDS[a] 2. Implement Evidence Act regulations and rule making 3. Identify legislation/regulatory priorities regarding CEP state-related recommendations 4. Develop data synchronization bill legislative strategy[b] 5. Identify legal options that would incentivize data holders to share data	1. Enact legal authorities for all necessary data-sharing entities 2. Adopt legal protections for private sector data sharing 3. Introduce legislative strategies/priorities

Governance framework and standards	1. Convene potential data-sharing organizations 2. Document current practices in data access 3. Catalog current data platforms of potential data-sharing organizations 4. Document current methods of data curation, protection, and preservation 5. Document existing metadata practices 6. Identify priorities for standards development 7. Draft data-sharing guidelines	1. Produce legislative language for governance procedures 2. Draft regulatory guidelines for practices 3. Convene relevant stakeholders to begin developing standards responding to infrastructure priorities 4. Establish governance roles and responsibilities
Transparency to the public	1. Identify communication priorities regarding transparency 2. Sponsor public discussion regarding alternative oversight structures to achieve transparency 3. Engage stakeholders to evaluate alternative approaches	1. Implement communication strategy that responds to stakeholders' priorities 2. Draft legislative language describing oversight vehicles to achieve transparency
State-of-the-art practices	1. Exchange knowledge about needed staff skillsets to support new operations of infrastructure 2. Build communities of practice to catalyze the technical skills base 3. Develop professional culture within pilot projects for data protection 4. Develop organizational procedures for continuous updating of tools and practices	1. Develop new partnerships across sectors to provide technical skills for all organizations involved 2. Continuously update procedures and practices to achieve goals of infrastructure

continued

TABLE 5-1 Continued

Attribute of New Data Infrastructure	Short-Term Tasks	Medium-Term Tasks
Organizations/ Partnerships	1. Monitor America's DataHub Consortium capabilities for collaborative research partnerships and data sharing 2. Clarify data infrastructure roles and responsibilities 3. Identify NSDS-provided services and capabilities 4. Clarify FSRDC services and capabilities 5. Sponsor bipartisan, multisector dialogue on how best to govern private sector data use for national statistical purposes 6. Expand voluntary private sector data sharing for statistical uses	1. (If NSDS is a portal) Begin pilots for accessing private sector data by connecting to data at data holder's site 2. (If new organization is developed for private sector data) Begin building the necessary governance framework and support 3. Scale up data-blending pilots to test the responsiveness of data service organizational capabilities 4. Identify challenges to be addressed and document benefits accruing to data holders

[a]The CHIPS and Science Act (PL 117-167) was signed into law on August 9, 2022. It allocates funding for an unnamed demonstration project to inform the establishment of NSDS.
[b]Such legislation would revise Internal Revenue Service regulations to allow the U.S. Census Bureau to share limited business tax data with the Bureau of Labor Statistics and the Bureau of Economic Analysis.

common good. This vision of a new data infrastructure assumes statistical agencies and approved researchers can access and blend data from multiple sources—to improve the quality, timeliness, granularity, and usefulness of statistics; to facilitate more rigorous social and economic research, and to support evidence-based policymaking and program evaluation. In this vision, effective and strengthened data safeguards will secure data, preserve privacy, and protect confidentiality while minimizing individual harm. Safeguard mechanisms and measures will be communicated and understood. The public and data holders will see how their data are used, by whom, for what purposes, and to what societal benefit, instilling confidence that their data will be used responsibly and ethically and only for approved statistical purposes. The public, data holders, data subjects, and other important constituencies will be engaged in standards development, data governance, and other decisions that affect them, strengthening trust in a new data infrastructure.

In the panel's opinion, a new data infrastructure should not only provide tangible benefits for the common good, but also ensure societal benefits proportionate to the possible costs and risks of acquiring and using a data asset. The panel's vision of a new data infrastructure supports the two-way flow of information from data holders to statistical agencies and back again. In the panel's view, statistical agencies should provide useful information and services back to data holders that inform data holders' decisions, operations, and activities. In turn, the public, data holders, and key stakeholders should support legislation and other changes that facilitate and support expanded data access and use.

References

Abraham, K.G., Haltiwanger, J.C., Hou, C., Sandusky, K., and Spletzer, J.R. (2021). Reconciling survey and administrative measures of self-employment. *Journal of Labor Economics, 39*(4), 825–860.

Advisory Committee on Data for Evidence Building. (2021). Year 1 Report (October 29, 2021). https://www.bea.gov/system/files/2021-10/acdeb-year-1-report.pdf

Alba, R. (2020). *The Great Demographic Illusion: Majority, Minority, and the Expanding American Mainstream.* Princeton University Press.

American Economic Association. (2021). How Data Sync Can Save US Official Statistics. https://www.aeaweb.org/content/file?id=15315

Arora, V. (2022). "Evidence Building and America's DataHub." Presentation at meeting of the Advisory Committee on Data for Evidence Building. January 21, 2022. https://www.bea.gov/system/files/2022-01/Arora-ACDEB-AmericasDataHub.pdf

Bahrampour, T. (2021). Census Bureau delays release of 5-year ACS data, citing pandemic. *Washington Post,* November 10. https://www.washingtonpost.com/dc-md-va/2021/11/10/2020-census-acs-delay/

Beauchamp, T.L., and Childress, J.F. (2001). Principles of Biomedical Ethics (5th ed.). Oxford University Press.

Bhaskar, R., Dillon, M., Foster, B., Knop, B., McBride, L., Perez-Patron, M., and Vickstrom, E. (2021). "Estimating SNAP Eligibility and Access Using Linked Survey and Administrative Records." Presentation at the Federal Committee on Statistical Methodology Annual Conference. November 4, 2021. https://copafs.org/wp-content/uploads/2021/11/H2Bhaskar.pptx

Biemer, P.P. (2010). Total survey error: Design, implementation, and evaluation. *Public Opinion Quarterly, 74*(5), 817–848.

Biemer, P.P., Groves, R.M., Lyberg, L.E., Mathiowitz, N.A., and Sudman, S. (2013). Measurement Errors in Surveys. John Wiley & Sons.

Bohman, M. (2021). "Health Care and Private-Sector Data: The Role of Private-Sector Data in the Health Care Sector." Presentation to the National Academies' Panel on The Scope, Components, and Key Characteristics of a 21st Century Data Infrastructure. December 9, 2021. https://www.nationalacademies.org/event/12-16-2021/docs/DBDC04350B8F03F-7C59C1BCE7C378E4A4EE5B942929F

Bowlby, G. (2021). "Private Sector Administrative Data and the Canadian Statistical System." Presentation to the National Academies' Panel on the Scope, Components, and Key Characteristics of a 21st Century Data Infrastructure. December 9, 2021. https://www.nationalacademies.org/event/12-09-2021/docs/DFD7AB9D5A0E38DE6E461557C33371D724BF52CAEB86

British Academy and the Royal Society. (2017). *Data Management and Use: Governance in the 21st Century*. https://royalsociety.org/-/media/policy/projects/data-governance/data-management-governance.pdf

Brown, A., Caporaso, A., Abraham, K.G., and Kreuter, F. (2018). *Findings from the Integrated Data Workshops Hosted by the Federal Committee on Statistical Methodology and Washington Statistical Society*. University of Maryland. https://nces.ed.gov/fcsm/pdf/Workshop_Summary.pdf

Buil-Gil, D., Solymosi, R., and Moretti, A. (2020). Nonparametric Bootstrap and Small Area Estimation to Mitigate Bias in Crowdsourced Data: Simulation Study and Application to Perceived Safety. *Big Data Meets Survey Science: A Collection of Innovative Methods*, 487–517. John Wiley & Sons.

Centers for Disease Control and Prevention. (2022). *Change in the Reporting of Marriage and Divorce Statistics*. National Vital Statistics System. https://www.cdc.gov/nchs/nvss/marriage-divorce.htm

Citro, C.F., Auerbach, J., Smith Evans, K., Groshen, E.L., Landefeld, J.S., Mulrow, J., Petska, T., Pierson, S., Potok, N., Rothwell, C.J., Thompson, J., Woodworth, J.L., and Wu, E. (2022). What protects the autonomy of the federal statistical agencies? An assessment of the procedures in place that protect the independence and objectivity of official statistics. *Statistics and Public Policy* (in press).

Commission on Evidence-Based Policymaking. (2017). *The Promise of Evidence-Based Policymaking: Report of the Commission on Evidence-Based Policymaking*. https://bipartisanpolicy.org/wp-content/uploads/2019/03/Full-Report-The-Promise-of-Evidence-Based-Policymaking-Report-of-the-Comission-on-Evidence-based-Policymaking.pdf_

Cunningham, J., Hui, A., Lane, J., and Putnam, G. (2022). A value-driven approach to building data infrastructures: The example of the Midwest Collaborative. *Harvard Data Science Review*, 4(1). https://hdsr.mitpress.mit.edu/pub/mfhpwpxq/release/2

Cutshall, C., and Lane, J. (2022). "Governance Focus Area." Presentation at the meeting of the Advisory Committee on Data for Evidence Building. March 18, 2022. https://www.bea.gov/system/files/2022-03/Governance-Report-Mar2022.pdf

Czajka, J.L., and Beyler, A. (2016). *Declining Response Rates in Federal Surveys: Trends and Implications (Background Paper)*. Washington, DC: Mathematica Policy Research. https://www.mathematica.org/publications/declining-response-rates-in-federal-surveys-trends-and-implications-background-paper

Czajka, J.L., and Stange, M. (2018). *Transparency in the Reporting of Quality for Integrated Data: A Review of International Standards and Guidelines*. Washington, DC: Mathematica, Policy Research. https://mathematica.org/publications/transparency-in-the-reporting-of-quality-for-integrated-data-a-review-of-international-standards

Darr, J. (2022). *New Tech, New Math, New Methods in Massive Upgrade of Census Bureau Construction Programs*. February 8, 2022. U.S. Census Bureau. https://www.census.gov/library/stories/2022/02/census-bureau-construction-data-from-stone-age-to-space-age.html

Datta, A.R., Ugarte, G., and Resnick, D. (2020). Linking Survey Data with Commercial or Administrative Data for Data Quality Assessment. *Big Data Meets Survey Science: A Collection of Innovative Methods*, 99–129. John Wiley & Sons.

Davies, T., Walker, S., Rubinstein, M., and Perini, F. (2019). *The State of Open Data: Histories and Horizons*. Cape Town and Ottawa: African Minds and International Development Research Centre. https://idl-bnc-idrc.dspacedirect.org/bitstream/handle/10625/57585/The%20State%20of%20Open%20Data.pdf?sequence=2&isAllowed=y

DeFrances, C.J., and Lau, D.T. (n.d.). *Collecting Electronic Health Record Data for the National Ambulatory Medical Care Survey and the National Hospital Care Survey*. Hyattsville, MD: National Center for Health Statistics. https://nces.ed.gov/FCSM/pdf/J4_DeFrances_2018FCSM.pdf

Deshpande, M., and Mueller-Smith, M.G. (2022). *Does Welfare Prevent Crime? The Criminal Justice Outcomes of Youth Removed from SSI*. NBER Working Paper 29800. National Bureau of Economic Research. http://www.nber.org/papers/w29800.pdf

Eticas Foundation. (2020). *Impact on Privacy and Data Protection of Citizen Science Projects*. https://eticasfoundation.org/governance/impact-on-privacy-and-data-protection-of-citizen-science-projects/

European Commission (n.d.) *European Data Strategy. Making the EU a Role Model for a Society Empowered by Data*. https://ec.europa.eu/info/strategy/priorities-2019-2024/europe-fit-digital-age/european-data-strategy

————. (2022). *Regulation of the European Parliament and of the Council on Harmonised Rules on Fair Access to and Use of Data (Data Act)*. https://digital-strategy.ec.europa.eu/en/library/data-act-proposal-regulation-harmonised-rules-fair-access-and-use-data

Federal CDO Council. (n.d.). *Working Group Data Inventory*. https://www.cdo.gov/data-inventory/

Federal Committee on Statistical Methodology. (2020). *A Framework for Data Quality*. FCSM 20-04. September, 2020. https://nces.ed.gov/fcsm/pdf/FCSM.20.04_A_Framework_for_Data_Quality.pdf

Federal Data Strategy. (n.d.). *Data Ethics Framework*. https://resources.data.gov/assets/documents/fds-data-ethics-framework.pdf

Federal Register. (1997). Order providing for the confidentiality of statistical information. 62 FR 35044. June 27, 1997. https://www.federalregister. gov/d/97-16934

————. (2011). Human subjects research protections: Enhancing protections for research subjects and reducing burden, delay, and ambiguity for investigators. 76 FR 44512. July 26, 2011. https://www.federalregister. gov/d/2011-18792

————. (2015). Federal policy for the protection of human subjects. 80 FR 53933. September 8, 2015. https://www.federalregister. gov/d/2015-21756

————. (2016). Agency information collection activities; request for comments; revision of the confidentiality pledge under Title 13 United States Code, Section 9. 81 FR 94321. December 23, 2016. https://www.federalregister.gov/d/2016-30959

————. (2017). Federal policy for the protection of human subjects. 82 FR 7149. January 19, 2017. https://www.federalregister. gov/d/2017-01058

————. (2022). The interagency council on statistical policy's recommendation for a standard application process (SAP) for requesting access to certain confidential data assets. 87 FR 2459. January 14, 2022. https://www.federalregister.gov/documents/2022/01/14/2022-00620/the-interagency-council-on-statistical-policys-recommendation-for-a-standard-application-process-sap

Finlay, K., Mueller-Smith, M.G., and Papp, J. (2022). *The Criminal Justice Administrative Records System: A Next-Generation Research Data Platform*. Criminal Justice Administrative Records System Working Paper. https://sites.lsa.umich.edu/mgms/wp-content/uploads/sites/283/2022/04/CJARS_Scientifiic_Data_article_20220408.pdf

Fischer, H.A., Gerber, L.R., and Wentz, E.A. (2021). Evaluating the fitness for use of citizen science data for wildlife monitoring. *Frontiers in Ecology and Evolution*, November 16, 2021. https://www.frontiersin.org/articles/10.3389/fevo.2021.620850/full

Fobia, A.C., Childs, J.H., and Eggleston, C. (2020). Attitudes Toward Data Linkage: Privacy. *Big Data Meets Survey Science: A Collection of Innovative Methods*, 683–712. John Wiley & Sons.

Gebru, T., Morgenstern, J., Vecchione, B., Wortman Vaughan, J., Wallach, H., Daumé III, H., and Crawford, K. (2021). Datasheets for datasets. *Communications of the ACM*, 64(12), 86–92.

Gee, M. (2021). "The Jobs and Employment Data Exchange." Presentation to the National Academies Panel on the Scope, Components, and Key Characteristics of a 21st Century Data Infrastructure. December 9, 2021. https://www.nationalacademies.org/event/12-09-2021/docs/DFC0803181C2CEE4C14F95764606900E4C9E5E84C1CC

Goodchild, M.F. (2007). Citizens as sensors: The world of volunteered geography. *GeoJournal*, 69, 211–221.

Grotpeter, J.K. (2007). Respondent Recall. *Handbook of Longitudinal Research Design, Measurement, and Analysis*, 109–122. Academic Press.

Groves, R.M., and Lyberg, L. (2010). Total survey error past, present, and future. *Public Opinion Quarterly*, 74(5), 849–879.

Groves, R.M., and Peytcheva, E. (2008). The impact of nonresponse rates on nonresponse bias: A meta-analysis. *Public Opinion Quarterly*, 72(Summer), 167–189.

Haltiwanger, J.C., Cafarella, M.J., Ehrlich, G., Jarmin, R.S., Johnson, D., and Shapiro, M.D. (2021). "RESET Project: Re-Engineering Statistics using Economic Transactions." Presentation to the National Academies' Panel on the Scope, Components, and Key Characteristics of a 21st Century Data Infrastructure. December 9, 2021. https://www.nationalacademies.org/event/12-09-2021/docs/D4C8E6E2696BAFD87311FBE547948D4A74401727C6F7

Hart, N., and Potok, N. (2020). *Modernizing U.S. Data Infrastructure: Design Considerations for Implementing a National Secure Data Service to Improve Statistics and Evidence Building*. Washington, DC: The Data Foundation. https://papers.ssrn.com/sol3/Delivery.cfm/SSRN_ID3700156_code4389785.pdf?abstractid=3700156&mirid=1

Hoeksema, M.J., Fienberg, H., and Jost, S. (2022). *America's Essential Data at Risk: A Vision to Preserve and Enhance the American Community Survey*. The Census Project (March). https://censusproject.files.wordpress.com/2022/03/census_white-paper_final_march_2022.pdf

Igo, S.E. (2018). *The Known Citizen: A History of Privacy in Modern America*. Harvard University Press.

ILR School. (2021). *Pandemic, Racial Inequities Underscore Need for Better Labor Market Data*. May 5, 2021. https://www.ilr.cornell.edu/work-and-coronavirus/public-policy/pandemic-racial-inequities-underscore-need-better-labor-market-data

Irby, L. (2022). *What Are the 3 Major Credit Reporting Agencies?* The Balance. February 12, 2022. https://www.thebalance.com/who-are-the-three-major-credit-bureaus-960416#:~:text=1%20Equifax.%20Equifax%20has%20been%20in%20business%20since,did%20not%20pay%20their%20bills.%203%20TransUnion.%20

Jarmin, R.S. (2019). Evolving measurement for an evolving economy: Thoughts on 21st century US economic statistics. *Journal of Economic Perspectives*, 33(1), 165–184.

Joint Center for Housing Studies. (2020). *Slight Gains in 2020 Outlook for Residential Remodeling*. Harvard University. January 16, 2020. https://www.jchs.harvard.edu/press-releases/slight-gains-2020-outlook-residential-remodeling

Kwan, M.P., Casas, I., and Schmitz, B.C. (2004). Protection of geoprivacy and accuracy of spatial information: How effective are geographical masks? *The International Journal for Geographic Information and Geovisualization*, 39(2), 15–28.

Lambert, L. (2022). Redfin: More sellers are cutting home prices as housing market demand begins to soften. *Fortune*, April 15, 2022. https://fortune.com/2022/04/15/housing-market-slowing-down-redfin-softening-mortgage-rates/

Latham & Watkins. (2016). What you need to know about the Cybersecurity Act of 2015. Client Alert Commentary, no. 1927. https: //www.lw.com/thoughtLeadership/lw-Cybersecurity-Act-of-2015

Lee-Ibarra, J. (2021). Data Equity: What Is It, and Why Does It Matter? JLI Consulting, July 10. https://www.jliconsultinghawaii.com/blog/2020/7/10/data-equity-what-is-it-and-why-does-it-matter

Liao, D., Berzofsky, M., Couzens Ianas, L., and Cooper A. (2020). Improving Quality of Administrative Data: A Case Study with FBI's National-Incident-Based Reporting System Data. *Big Data Meets Survey Science: A Collection of Innovative Methods*, 217–243. John Wiley & Sons.

Market Research Store. (2021). *ICT Market – Global Industry Research Analysis*. https://www.marketresearchstore.com/market-insights/ict-market-805765

Markle Foundation. (2021). *Unlocking Responsible Access to Data to increase Equity and Economic Mobility*. https://markle.org/app/uploads/2022/03/Unlocking-Responsible-Access-to-Data.pdf

Marten, A. (2022). "The Evidence Act's Standard Application Process." Presentation at meeting of the Advisory Committee on Data for Evidence Building. January 21, 2022. https://www.bea.gov/system/files/2022-01/Marten-ICSP-Presentation-to-ACDEB-1-18-22.pdf

Marwick, A.E., and boyd, d. (2014). Networked privacy: How teenagers negotiate context in social media. *New Media & Society, 16*(7), 1051–1067.

Melendez, S., and Pasternac, A. (2019). Here are the data brokers quietly buying and selling your personal information. *Fast Company*, March 2. https://www.fastcompany.com/90310803/here-are-the-data-brokers-quietly-buying-and-selling-your-personal-information

Moyer, B. (2021). "Private-Sector Health Data: Overview of Data Infrastructure, Initiatives, & Lessons Learned." Presentation to the National Academies' Panel on the Scope, Components, and Key Characteristics of a 21st Century Data Infrastructure. December 16, 2021. https://www.nationalacademies.org/event/12-16-2021/docs/D668C778936FB43CD-9F9E24040531F742FF9FCB9886A

National Academies of Sciences, Engineering, and Medicine. (2017a). *Federal Statistics, Multiple Data Sources, and Privacy Protection: Next Steps*. The National Academies Press.

———. (2017b). *Innovations in Federal Statistics: Combining Data Sources While Protecting Privacy*. The National Academies Press.

———. (2021). *Principles and Practices for a Federal Statistical Agency, Seventh Edition*. The National Academies Press. https://doi.org/10.17226/25885

———. (2022a). *Transparency in Statistical Information for the National Center for Science and Engineering Statistics and All Federal Statistical Agencies*. The National Academies Press.

———. (2022b). *A Vision and Roadmap for Education Statistics*. The National Academies Press. https://doi.org/10.17226/26392

National Archives. (2021). Using the National Archives catalog. https://www.archives.gov/research/catalog/help/using

National Institutes of Health. (2022). *NIH's All of Us Research Program Releases First Genomic Dataset of Nearly 100,000 Whole Genome Sequences*. March 17, 2022. https://www.nih.gov/news-events/news-releases/nih-s-all-us-research-program-releases-first-genomic-dataset-nearly-100000-whole-genome-sequences

National Research Council (NRC). (2003) *Protecting Participants and Facilitating Social and Behavioral Sciences Research.* Panel on Institutional Review Boards, Surveys, and Social Science Research, C.F. Citro, D.R. Ilgen, and C.B. Marrett, eds. Committee on National Statistics and Board on Behavioral,Cognitive, and Sensory Sciences. Washington D.C" The National Academies Press. https://doi.org/10.17226/10638

_____. (2014). *Proposed Revisions to the Common Rule for the Protection of Human Subjects in the Behavioral and Social Sciences.* Committee on Revisions to the Common Rule for the Protection of Human Subjects in Research in the Behavioral and Social Sciences, Board on Behavioral, Cognitive, and Sensory Sciences, Committee on National Statistics, and Committee on Population. The National Academies Press https://doi.org/10.17226/18614

O'Connor, N. (2018). *Reforming the U.S. Approach to Data Protection and Privacy.* Council on Foreign Relations, Digital and Cyberspace Policy Program. January 30, 2018. https://www.cfr.org/report/reforming-us-approach-data-protection

Organisation for Economic Co-operation and Development. (2019). *Institutions Guaranteeing Access to Information: OECD and MENA Region.* https://www.oecd-ilibrary.org/governance/institutions-guaranteeing-access-to-information_e6d58b52-en

Osano. (2020). *Data Privacy Laws: What You Need to Know in 2022.* June 14, 2020. https://www.osano.com/articles/data-privacy-laws

Page, E.T., Young, S.K., Sweitzer, M.D., and Okrent, A.M. (2021). "Determining Household Obesity Status Using Scanner Data." Presentation at the 2021 AAEA & WAEA Joint Annual Meeting, Austin TX. https://ageconsearch.umn.edu/record/312785/files/Abstracts_21_06_15_15_11_43_90__199_136_105_37_0.pdf

Potok, N., and Hart, N. (2022). A Blueprint for Implementing the National Secure Data Service: Initial Governance and Administrative Priorities for the National Science Foundation. The Data Foundation, Washington, DC. https://www.datafoundation.org/a-blueprint-for-implementing-the-national-secure-data-service-2022

Pozen, D. (2018). Transparency's ideological drift. *The Yale Law Journal,* 128, 100–165.

Prewitt, K., (2013). *What Is "Your" Race?: The Census and Our Flawed Efforts to Classify Americans.* Princeton University Press.

Privacy Bee. (2021). *These Are the Largest Data Brokers in America.* https://privacybee.com/blog/these-are-the-largest-data-brokers-in-america/

Rao, J., and Prasad, N. (1986). Discussion: Jackknife, bootstrap and other resampling methods in regression analysis. *The Annals of Statistics,* 14(4), 1320–1322.

Reamer, A. (2021). "Federal Statistical Agency Uses of Private Sector Data: Study Findings to Date." Presentation to the National Academies' Panel on the Scope, Components, and Key Characteristics of a 21st Century Data Infrastructure. December 9, 2021. https://www.nationalacademies.org/event/12-09-2021/docs/D9B3CF5B91DDB9DF7FD2E270029E54A38A98AE27B7B6

Ruhaak, A. (2019). Data Trusts: Why, What and How. *Medium,* November 11, 2019. https://medium.com/@anoukruhaak/data-trusts-why-what-and-how-a8b53b53d34

Snijkers, G., Haraldsen, G., Jones, J., and Willimack, D.K. (2013*).* Designing and Conducting Business Surveys. John Wiley & Sons.

Statista. (2022). *Residential Improvements in The United States from 2005 to 2021, with Forecasts from 2022 to 2026.* https://www.statista.com/statistics/604682/value-of-us-residential-building-improvement-construction/

Statistics Canada. (2015). *Statistics Canada Policy on the Use of Administrative Data Obtained under the Statistics Act.* https://www.statcan.gc.ca/en/about/policy/admin_data

_____. (2021). *Requests for Information – Prices and Price Indexes.* https://www.statcan.gc.ca/en/our-data/where/admin-rfi/prices-price-indexes

Stevens, J. (2021). "Federal Reserve Board Experience Using Transaction Data." Presentation to the National Academies' Panel on the Scope, Components, and Key Characteristics of a 21st Century Data Infrastructure. December 9, 2021. https://www.nationalacademies. org/event/12-09-2021/docs/D621B5C5E61EBE2489A00AC98C86D5CC096F7CE3BA62

Studds, S. (2021). "Blended Data in the Census Bureau's Monthly State Retail Sales Data Product." Presentation to the National Academies' Panel on the Scope, Components, and Key Characteristics of a 21st Century Data Infrastructure. December 9, 2021. https://www.nationalacademies. org/event/12-09-2021/docs/DBA437A832BAE8FF4072013340D57EED2F46017EE82D

Sweeney, L., Yoo, J.S., Perovich, L., Boronow, K.E., Brown, P., and Brody, J.G. (2017). Re-identification risks in HIPAA Safe Harbor data: A study of data from one environmental health study. *Technology Science*. https://techscience.org/a/2017082801/

Tam, S.M., Kim, J.K., Ang, L., and Pham, H. (2020). Mining the New Oil for Official Statistics. *Big Data Meets Survey Science: A Collection of Innovative Methods*, 339–357. John Wiley & Sons.

U.K. Department for Digital, Culture, Media, & Sport. (2019). *National Data Strategy*. https://www.gov.uk/guidance/national-data-strategy

U.K. Statistics Authority. (2022a). Five Year Strategy: Statistics for the public good: Informing the UK. Improving Lives. Building the Future. https://uksa.statisticsauthority.gov.uk/ wp-content/uploads/2020/07/UKSA-Strategy-2020.pdf

U.K. Statistics Authority. (2022b). About the Authority. https://uksa.statisticsauthority.gov. uk/about-the-authority/

U.S. Bureau of Labor Statistics. (n.d.). Mass Layoff Statistics. https://www.bls.gov/mls/

_____. (2021). Quarterly Census of Employment and Wages. https://www.bls.gov/cew/ overview.htm

_____. (2022). *Household and Establishment Survey Response Rates*. Office of Survey Methods Research. https://www.bls.gov/osmr/response-rates/

U.S. Census Bureau. (n.d.). Title 13 U.S. Code. https://www.census.gov/history/www/reference/ privacy_confidentiality/title_13_us_code.html

_____. (2007). *Residential Improvements and Repairs*. https://www.census.gov/construc-tion/c50/c50index.html#:~:text=Announcements%20The%20U.S.%20Census%20 Bureau%20has%20discontinued%20the,last%20report%20of%20residential%20 improvements%20and%20repairs%20data

_____. (2021a). *Census Bureau Announces Changes for 2020 American Community Survey 1-Year Estimates*. https://www.census.gov/newsroom/press-releases/2021/changes-2020-acs-1-year.html

_____. (2021b). *2020 ACS 1-Year Experimental Data Release*. https://www.census.gov/ programs-surveys/acs/data/experimental-data.html

_____. (2021c). 2020 ACS 1-Year Estimates What You Need to Know. July, 2021. https:// www.census.gov/programs-surveys/acs/library/flyers/flow-chart.html

_____. (2021d). Survey of Income and Program Participation. https://www.census.gov/ history/www/programs/demographic/survey_of_income_and_program_participation.html

U.S. Congress. (1974). The Privacy Act of 1974. P.L. 93-579. https://www.archives.gov/about/ laws/privacy-act-1974.html

_____. (1995). Paperwork Reduction Act. P.L. 104-13. https://www.congress.gov/104/ plaws/publ13/PLAW-104publ13.pdf

_____. (1996). Health Insurance Portability and Accountability Act of 1996. P.L. 104-191. https://www.govinfo.gov/content/pkg/PLAW-104publ191/pdf/PLAW-104publ191.pdf

_____. (2002a). The E-Government Act of 2002. P.L. 107-347. https://www.congress. gov/107/plaws/publ347/PLAW-107publ347.pdf

_____. (2002b). Confidential Information Protection and Statistical Efficiency Act of 2002. H.R. 5215. https://www.congress.gov/bill/107th-congress/house-bill/5215#:~:text= Confidential%20Information%20Protection%20and%20Statistical%20Efficiency%20 Act%20of%202002%20%2D%20Requires,to%20this%20Act%20to%20be

_____. (2019). Foundations for Evidence-Based Policymaking Act of 2018. P.L. 115-435. https://www.congress.gov/bill/115th-congress/house-bill/4174/text

_____. (2021). National Science Foundation for the Future Act. H.R. 2225. https://www. congress.gov/bill/117th-congress/house-bill/2225

_____. (2022a). CHIPS and Science Act of 2022. P.L. 117-167. https://science.house.gov/ imo/media/doc/the_chips_and_science_act.pdf

_____. (2022b). Confidentiality and Disclosure of Returns and Return Information. 26 USC 6103. https://uscode.house.gov/view.xhtml?req=(title:26%20section:6103%20 edition:prelim)#codification-note

U.S. Department of Commerce, Bureau of Economic Analysis. (2022). Advisory Committee on Data for Evidence Building. https://www.bea.gov/evidence

U.S. Government Accountability Office. (2020). *Internet of Things: Information on Use by Federal Agencies*. GAO-20-577. https://www.gao.gov/assets/gao-20-577.pdf

U.S. Office of Management and Budget (OMB). (2003). OMB Guidance for Implementing the Privacy Provisions of the E-Government Act of 2002, Memorandum (M-03-22). September 26, 2003. https://georgewbush-whitehouse.archives.gov/omb/memoranda/ m03-22.html

_____. (2016). Supplemental guidance on the implementation of M-15-14 "Management and oversight of federal information technology"—Applying FITARA common baseline to statistical agencies and units. Memorandum from Tony Scott, Federal Chief Information Officer, and Howard Shelanski, Administrator, Office of Regulatory Affairs. https:// management.cio.gov/assets/docs/FITARA_Guidance_Statistical_Agencies_and_Units_ OMB.pdf

_____. (2019). Phase 1 Implementation of the Foundations for Evidence-Based Policymaking Act of 2018: Learning Agendas, Personnel, and Planning Guidance, Memorandum M-19-23. July 10, 2019. https://www.whitehouse.gov/wp-content/uploads/2019/07/M-19-23. pdf

Valentino-DeVries, J., Singer, N., Keller, M.H., and Krolik, A. (2018). Your Apps Know Where You Were Last Night, and They're Not Keeping It Secret. *The New York Times*, December 10.

Voorheis, J. (2021). "Measuring the Distributional Effects of Climate Change and Environmental Inequality with Linked Survey, Census and Administrative Data." Presentation at the Federal Committee on Statistical Methodology Annual Conference. November 2, 2021. https://copafs.org/wp-content/uploads/2021/11/C5Voorheis.pptx

The White House. (2021a). Restoring Trust in Government Through Scientific Integrity and Evidence-Based Policymaking, Memorandum. January 27, 2021. https://www.whitehouse. gov/briefing-room/presidential-actions/2021/01/27/memorandum-on-restoring-trust-in-government-through-scientific-integrity-and-evidence-based-policymaking/

_____. (2021b). Executive Order on Advancing Racial Equity and Support for Underserved Communities Through the Federal Government. January 20, 2021. https://www.white-house.gov/briefing-room/presidential-actions/2021/01/20/executive-order-on-advancing-racial-equity-and-support-for-underserved-communities-through-the-federal-government/

_____. (2022a). Fact Sheet: Biden-Harris Administration Announces New Initiative to Improve Supply Chain Data Flow. March 15, 2022. https://www.whitehouse.gov/ briefing-room/statements-releases/2022/03/15/fact-sheet-biden-harris-administration-announces-new-initiative-to-improve-supply-chain-data-flow/

_____. (2022b). A Vision for Equitable Data: Recommendations from the Equitable Data Working Group. https://www.whitehouse.gov/wp-content/uploads/2022/04/eo13985-vision-for-equitable-data.pdf

Willkie, Farr, and Gallagher, LLP. (n.d.). State Data Broker Laws. https://complianceconcourse.willkie.com/resources/privacy-and-cybersecurity-us-state-data-broker-laws

Wright, T. (2021). The Platform Transparency and Accountability Act: New legislation addresses platform data secrecy. Stanford Cyber Policy Center. December 9, 2021. https://cyber.fsi.stanford.edu/news/platform-transparency-and-accountability-act-new-legislation-addresses-platform-data-secrecy

Appendix A

Biographical Sketches of Panel Members

Robert M. Groves (*Chair,* he/him) is executive vice president and provost of Georgetown University, where he is also the Gerard J. Campbell professor in the Department of Mathematics and Statistics as well as a professor in the Department of Sociology. Before joining Georgetown as provost, he served as director of the U.S. Census Bureau, appointed by President Barack Obama. Previously, he was director of the University of Michigan Survey Research Center and research professor at the Joint Program in Survey Methodology at the University of Maryland. He also served as associate director for research and methodology for the U.S. Census Bureau. His research focuses on the effects of the mode of data collection on responses in sample surveys, the social and political influences on survey participation, the use of adaptive research designs to improve the cost and error properties of statistics, and how public privacy concerns affect attitudes toward statistical agencies. He is an elected member of the National Academy of Sciences and the National Academy of Medicine. He has been chair of the National Academies' Committee on National Statistics (CNSTAT), served as a member of CNSTAT and as a member of Division of Behavioral and Social Sciences and Education as well as on numerous National Academies' boards, panels, and committees, including chair of the Panel on Improving Federal Statistics for Policy and Social Science Research Using Multiple Data Sources and State-of-the-Art Estimation Methods. He is an elected fellow of the American Statistical Association and an elected member of the International Statistical Institute and the American Academy of Arts and Sciences. He has an A.B. in sociology from Dartmouth College and an M.A. and Ph.D. in sociology from the University of Michigan.

danah boyd (she/her) is a partner researcher at Microsoft Research, the founder of the research institute Data & Society, and a visiting professor at New York University's Interactive Telecommunications Program. Her research blends science and technology studies, sociology, and computer science to examine how society shapes and is shaped by sociotechnical systems, with an eye on how inequity and societal values manifest in algorithmic and data-oriented systems. She is the author of *It's Complicated: The Social Lives of Networked Teens and Participatory Culture in a Networked Era*. She is the chairperson of the board of Crisis Text Line, a director of Crisis Text Line, and a member of the Council on Foreign Relations. She has received numerous awards, including the Electronic Frontier Foundation's Pioneer/Barlow Award, the American Sociological Association's Communication and Information Technology Public Sociology Award, MIT Tech Review's TR35, and a Young Global Leader of the World Economic Forum. She holds a B.S. in computer science from Brown University, an M.A. in media arts from the MIT Media Lab, and a Ph.D. from the School of Information, University of California, Berkeley.

Anne C. Case (she/her) is the Alexander Stewart 1886 professor of economics and public affairs emerita at Princeton University. She is also the director of the Research Program in Development Studies at Princeton. Her current research examines the relationship between economic status and health status over the life course in developed and developing countries. Her research on midlife morbidity and mortality is summarized in her book *Deaths of Despair and the Future of Capitalism*. She is a current member of the National Academies' Committee on National Statistics and previously served on the Committee on Population (CPOP) in the Division of Behavioral and Social Sciences and Education. She served on the National Institutes of Health's National Research Advisory Council, Child Health and Human Development, and the President's Committee on the National Medal of Science. She is an elected member of the American Philosophical Society, the American Academy of Arts and Sciences, the National Academy of Sciences, and the National Academy of Medicine. She has a B.S. from the State University of New York, Albany, an M.P.A. from Princeton University, and a Ph.D. in economics from Princeton University.

Janet Currie (she/her) is the Henry Putnam professor of economics and public affairs at Princeton University and director of Princeton's Center for Health and Wellbeing. Her research focuses on the impact of government policies and poverty on the health and well-being of children over their life cycles. She has written about early intervention programs and expansions of the Medicaid program, public housing, and food and nutrition programs. Her current research focuses on socioeconomic differences in child health and environmental threats to children's health. She is a member of the National Academy of Medicine. She currently serves on the National Academies' Committee on National Statistics and previously on the Board on Children, Youth, and Families and the Committee on Population. She has served on several National Academies' ad hoc committees on the promotion of the well-being of children and families. She is currently on the Board of Reviewing Editors of *Science* magazine and the editorial board of the *Quarterly Journal of Economics*. She has been elected to membership positions in numerous professional associations, including a member of the American Academy of Arts and Sciences, a member of the American Academy of Political and Social Sciences, and a fellow of the Econometric Society. She served as both president and vice president of the Society of Labor Economists, and as vice president of the American Economic Association. She has a B.A. and M.A. in economics from the University of Toronto and a Ph.D. from Princeton University.

Erica L. Groshen (she/her) is a senior labor economics advisor at Cornell University-ILR, a research fellow at the Upjohn Institute for Employment Research, and a member of the Federal Economic Statistics Advisory Council. She served as 14th Commissioner of the U.S. Bureau of Labor Statistics, the principal federal agency responsible for measuring labor market activity, working conditions, and inflation. Before that, she was vice president of the Research and Statistics Group of the Federal Reserve Bank of New York. Her research centers on employers' roles in labor market outcomes. She co-edited *Improving Employment and Earnings in Twenty-First Century Labor Markets*, co-authored *How New Is the "New Employment Contract"?* and co-edited *Structural Changes in U.S. Labor Markets: Causes and Consequences*. She is a member of the National Academies' Committee on National Statistics. Groshen received the Susan C. Eaton Outstanding Scholar-Practitioner Award from the Labor and Employment Relations Association and was appointed a fellow of the American Statistical Association. She holds a B.S. in mathematics and economics from the University of Wisconsin-Madison and a Ph.D. in economics from Harvard University.

Margaret C. Levenstein (she/her) is the director of the Inter-university Consortium for Political and Social Research (ICPSR) at the University of Michigan, a professor at the School of Information, a research professor at the Institute for Social Research, and an adjunct professor of business economics and public policy at the Ross School of Business at the University of Michigan. Levenstein first joined ICPSR's Survey Research Center as executive director of the Michigan Census Research Data Center, a joint project with the U.S. Census Bureau. She has taken an active role at ICPSR, joining the Director's Advisory Committee on Diversity, serving as chair of

ICPSR's diversity, equity, and inclusion strategic planning committee, and serving as the liaison to the larger university program. Levenstein's research and teaching interests include industrial organization, competition policy, business history, data confidentiality protection, and the improvement of economic statistics. She is associate chair of the American Economic Association's Committee on the Status of Women in the Economics Profession and past president of the Business History Conference. Levenstein has a B.A. from Barnard College, Columbia University, and a Ph.D. in economics from Yale University.

Ted McCann (he/him) is vice president for programs and policies at the American Idea Foundation, where he engages third-party organizations to ensure that evidence is fully utilized in the federal policy-making process. He was previously on staff to the U.S. Congress as a senior advisor to the Speaker of the House, staff director of the House Ways and Means Social Security Subcommittee, and an analyst with the House Budget Committee. He negotiated and drove the passage of dozens of pieces of legislation, including passage of the Evidence Act, the first Federal Communications Commission reauthorization bill in over two decades, criminal justice reform, and improvements to the Social Security Administration's finances. He developed a strategy for the most extensive use of the Congressional Review Act in history and helped spearhead former speaker Paul Ryan's Better Way agenda and the Roadmap for America's Future. In addition to studying at the Naval War College, he holds a B.A. in foreign affairs and economics from Miami University.

C. Matthew Snipp (he/him) is Burnet C. and Milfred Finley Wohlford professor of sociology at Stanford University, where he currently serves as director of the Secure Data Center, deputy director of the Institute for Research in the Social Sciences, and chair of the Native American Studies program. He has written extensively on American Indians, focusing specifically on the interaction of American Indians and the U.S. census. He is a member of the National Academies' Committee on National Statistics. Previously, he served as a member of the Panel to Review the 2010 Census, the Panel on Residence Rules in the Decennial Census, the Panel on the Research on Future Census Methods, and as co-chair of the Steering Committee for a Workshop on Developing a New National Survey on Social Mobility. He has also served on the U.S. Census Bureau's Technical Advisory Committee on Racial and Ethnic Statistics and the Native American Population Advisory Committee. He is the former director of the Center for Comparative Studies of Race and Ethnicity. Before moving to Stanford, he was associate professor and professor of rural sociology at the University of Wisconsin–Madison, where he held affiliate appointments with several other units, and assistant and associate professor of sociology at the University of Maryland. He has an M.S. and Ph.D. in sociology from the University of Wisconsin, Madison.

Patricia Solís (she/her) is executive director of the Knowledge Exchange for Resilience and an associate research professor of geography in the School of Geographical Sciences and Urban Planning, both at Arizona State University (ASU). The Knowledge Exchange for Resilience is a campus-wide effort to link multisector community needs with research innovations in building community resilience. Her research focuses on applications of open geospatial technologies to address socially relevant challenges, from water resource conflict to climate change-induced hazards to broadening participation in higher education. Solís is co-founder and director of YouthMappers, a consortium of student-led chapters on more than 208 university campuses in 48 countries, which create and use open spatial data for humanitarian and development needs in collaboration with the U.S. Agency for International Development. Prior to joining ASU, she was co-director of the Center for Geospatial Technology at Texas Tech University and deputy director and director of research at the American Association of Geographers. She was awarded Ronald F. Abler Distinguished Service Honors from the American Association of Geographers. Solís received a B.S. in physics, a B.A. in German, and an M.A. in geography from Kansas State University. She holds a Ph.D. in geography from the University of Iowa.

Appendix B

Workshop Agendas

WORKSHOP 1, DECEMBER 9, 2021:
SESSIONS 1–3

11:00 am Welcome, Introductions, and Workshop Goals
- **Robert Groves,** *Chair,* Georgetown University
- **Cheryl Eavey,** National Science Foundation

11:15 am Session 1: Data Infrastructure Initiatives—Description and Discussion

Moderators:
- **Robert Groves,** Georgetown University
- **Patricia Solis,** Arizona State University

This session will discuss current initiatives to improve the U.S. data infrastructure, including the accomplishments and future activities of the Advisory Committee on Data for Evidence Building, the Interagency Council on Statistical Policy initiative related to uses of private sector data by federal statistical agencies, and the NSF-sponsored CNSTAT data infrastructure initiative.

Overview of Data Infrastructure Initiatives & Lessons Learned
- Accomplishments and Future Plans of the Advisory Committee on Data for Evidence Building: **Emilda Rivers,** National Center for Science and Engineering Statistics and ACDEB chair
- Initiative on Uses of Private Sector Data at the Interagency Council on Statistical Policy: **Andrew Reamer,** George Washington University
- CNSTAT Data Infrastructure Initiative: **Robert Groves,** Georgetown University

Panel Discussion—Lessons Learned, Opportunities, Challenges, and Next Steps

- **Ivan Deloach,** Federal Geographic Data Committee
- **Mathew Shapiro,** University of Michigan
- **John Stevens,** Federal Reserve Board of Governors

1:00 pm   *Break*

1:15 pm   Session 2: Private Sector Data Uses for National Statistical Purposes—International Perspectives

Moderators:
- **Matt Snipp,** Stanford University
- **Ted McCann,** American Idea Foundation

International experts will share their perspectives and lessons learned from integrating private sector statistics into national statistical programs. The focus will be on identifying aids and impediments to using private sector data, strategies used to overcome obstacles and gain private sector support, and what, in retrospect, they would do differently.

- **Antonio Chessa,** Statistics Netherlands
- **Sarah Henry,** UK Office of National Statistics
- **Geoff Bowlby,** Statistics Canada

2:30 pm   *Break*

2:45 pm   Session 3: Federal Statistical Agencies' Uses of Private Sector Transaction Data

Moderators:
- **Erica Groshen,** Cornell University
- **Margaret Levenstein,** University of Michigan

The presenters will focus on the acquisition process, aids and impediments, lessons learned, and key changes that would have improved project success.

- Monthly State Retail Sales Experimental Data Product: **Stephanie Studds,** U.S. Census Bureau
- Jobs and Employment Data Exchange (JEDx): **Matt Gee,** Brighthive
- Re-Engineering Key National Economic Indicators **John Haltiwanger,** University of Maryland
- Federal Reserve Board Experience Using Transaction Data: **John Stevens,** Federal Reserve Board of Governors

4:30 pm   Reactions and Wrap-Up
Moderator:
- **Robert Groves,** Georgetown University

5:00 pm   **Adjournment**

WORKSHOP 2, DECEMBER 16, 2021: SESSIONS 4–5

11:00 am   Welcome, Introductions, and Workshop Goals
- **Robert Groves,** *Chair,* Georgetown University

11:10 am   Session 4: Federal Statistical Agencies' and Non-Profits' Use of Private Sector Health Data

Moderators:
- **Janet Currie,** Princeton University
- **Anne Case,** Princeton University

Overview of Data Infrastructure Initiatives & Lessons Learned
- Health Satellite Accounts at the Bureau of Economic Analysis: **Mary Bohman,** Bureau of Economic Analysis

- National Center for Health Statistics Initiatives to Use Private Sector Data:
  Brian Moyer, National Center for Health Statistics
- The Health Care Cost Institute:
  Niall Brennan, President and CEO

12:20 pm   *Break*

12:30 pm   Session 5: Perspectives on Using Private Sector Data for Official Statistics and Research

Moderators:
- **danah boyd,** Data & Society
- **Helen Nissenbaum,** Cornell Tech
- **Ted McCann,** American Idea Foundation

Conversation about Social Science One
- Lessons learned, impediments, what could have been done differently, and context for legislative proposal.
  Nathan Persily, Stanford Law School

1:00 pm   Description of the Changing Legal/Regulatory/Privacy Landscape Regarding Private Sector Data

The objective is to inform the panel about the changing political landscape regarding laws, regulations, and privacy and how these changes may impact panel deliberations.
- **Salome Viljoen,** Columbia Law School

1:30 pm   Data Exchange as a Gift: An Argument and Reactions
- Introduction and Presentation
  danah boyd, Data & Society

- Reaction and Feedback (5–7 minutes initial reactions followed by questions)
- Precision medicine perspective
  Kadija Ferryman, Johns Hopkins Public Health
- Business perspective
  Frank Nothaft, CoreLogic
- Policy perspective
  DJ Patil, Devoted Health (former chief data scientist, U.S. Office of Science and Technology Policy)

- Statistical system perspective
  Katherine Wallman (former chief statistician, U.S. Office
  of Management and Budget)
- Business perspective
  Maurine Haver, Haver Analytics

2:50 pm   Reactions and Wrap-Up
            Moderator:
            - **Robert Groves,** Georgetown University

3:00 pm   Adjournment